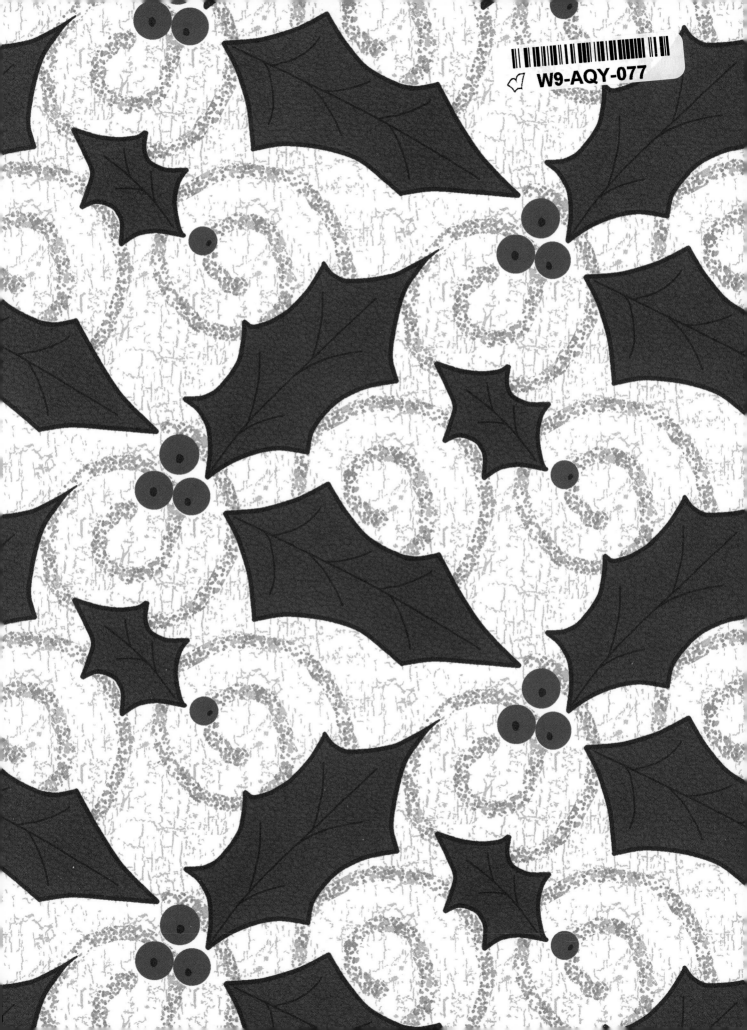

W9-AQY-077

Better Homes and Gardens®

Better Homes and Gardens® Books
Des Moines, Iowa

Better Homes and Gardens®
Celebrate the Season® 2004
Editor: Vicki Ingham
Project Manager/Writer: Jilann Severson
Contributing Editor/Writer: Winifred Moranville
Contributing Art Director/Graphic Designer: Marisa Dirks
Copy Chief: Terri Fredrickson
Publishing Operations Manager: Karen Schirm
Book Production Managers: Pam Kvitne, Marjorie J. Schenkelberg, Rick von Holdt, Mark Weaver
Contributing Copy Editor: Judy Friedman
Contributing Proofreaders: Becky Danley, Gretchen Kauffman, Donna Segal
Indexer: Stephanie Reymann
Editorial Assistants: Cheryl Eckert, Kaye Chabot
Edit and Design Production Coordinator: Mary Lee Gavin

Meredith® Books
Editor in Chief: Linda Raglan Cunningham
Design Director: Matt Strelecki
Managing Editor: Gregory H. Kayko
Executive Editor, Food and Crafts: Jennifer Dorland Darling

Publisher: James D. Blume
Executive Director, Marketing: Jeffrey Myers
Executive Director, New Business Development: Todd M. Davis
Executive Director, Sales: Ken Zagor
Director, Operations: George A. Susral
Director, Production: Douglas M. Johnston
Business Director: Jim Leonard

Vice President and General Manager: Douglas J. Guendel

Better Homes and Gardens® Magazine
Editor in Chief: Karol DeWulf Nickell
Deputy Editor, Home Design: Oma Blaise Ford
Deputy Editor, Food and Entertaining: Nancy Hopkins

Meredith Publishing Group
President, Publishing Group: Stephen M. Lacy
Vice President-Publishing Director: Bob Mate

Meredith Corporation
Chairman and Chief Executive Officer: William T. Kerr

In Memoriam: E. T. Meredith III (1933-2003)

All of us at Meredith® Books are dedicated to providing you with information and ideas to enhance your home. We welcome your comments and suggestions. Write to us at: Meredith Books, Food and Crafts Editorial Department, 1716 Locust St., Des Moines, IA 50309-3023.

If you would like to purchase any of our home decorating and design, cooking, crafts, gardening, or home improvement books, check wherever quality books are sold. Or visit us at: bhgbooks.com
Cover Photograph: Peter Krumhardt

Our seal assures you that every recipe in *Celebrate the Season 2004* has been tested in the Better Homes and Gardens® Test Kitchen. This means that each recipe is practical and reliable, and meets our high standards of taste appeal. We guarantee your satisfaction with this book for as long as you own it.

Copyright © 2004 by Meredith Corporation, Des Moines, Iowa. First Edition.
All rights reserved. Printed in the United States of America.
ISSN: 1098-0733. ISBN: 0-696-22124-1

holidays

have a way of sneaking up on you. Yesterday was the Fourth of July. How can Thanksgiving be just around the corner? As you zip from task to task, you still crave time to be creative. That seems especially true at the holidays. Our editorial team challenged designers to come up with projects and ideas that were quick and easy but would still give you great results. They came through in ways we could have never imagined, providing you with fantastic designs for decorating, entertaining, and gift ideas that extend from autumn to New Year's. For your holiday entertaining, check out the multicultural potluck (page 76) that is a celebration of diversity and the family New Year's party (page 96) that guarantees good times for everyone. As a special bonus, see the decorative papers on the inside covers and on page 154 and a calligraphy alphabet on page 156 that are available only in this book. From cover to cover, you'll find clever ideas that let you be creative and still have time to relax and savor the season.

— Jilann Severson

Ornament Centerpiece

■ Create an elegant centerpiece in a matter of minutes. Pile a holiday bowl or compote high with ornaments and garlands in a single color scheme. Vary the textures, finishes, and sizes of ornaments for interest and use only one hue to give the arrangement more impact. Fill in any bare spots and steady the balls with bead garland.

table *of* contents

setting the stage

page 6 Give your home a holiday feel from autumn through New Year's with pillows, window treatments, table linens, wreaths, ornaments, and other trims that reflect the colors and motifs of each season.

gathering together

page 56 Share your celebrations with family and friends using recipes and table settings that reflect your holiday spirit. An ethnic potluck and a family New Year's party ensure there will be parties for one and all.

5

giving from the heart

page 124 Handmade and heartfelt are one and the same when gifts are crafted with someone special in mind. Here you will find a selection of holiday gifts as well as those that are guaranteed to be used year-round.

just for kids

page 144 Keep your spirits bright with whimsical gifts and ornaments made just for—and just by—kids. You'll have fun crafting for ages from toddlers to teens.

In a Twinkling

Easy-to-do ideas for the holidays

Hearty Christmas Greetings

setting the stage

Bring warmth and

SETTING *the* STAGE

oy to your home this season with decorative touches made from simple-to-gather items. Whether your style is lush and lavish, fun and funky, or simply sophisticated, on the following pages you'll find wreaths, ornaments, window treatments, pillows, and a host of other decorations that add a relaxing feel as you welcome family and friends.

autumnal appliqué

Bring warmth to
crisp fall days
with patchwork
made from old wool
clothing and
appliquéd with
richly colored leaves.

What You'll Need...

- [ ] Various colors and patterns of wool clothing
- [ ] Matching threads and tapestry yarns
- [ ] 2½ yards of navy and teal wool felt
- [ ] Pinking shears
- [ ] 2½-inch diameter lid
- [ ] Light-colored fabric marker or chalk
- [ ] Gathered leaves
- [ ] ¼ yard each of several colors of wool felt for the appliquéd leaves
- [ ] Tapestry needle
- [ ] ¾-inch-wide grosgrain ribbon for chair tiebacks

table runner

1 Cut up the clothing, removing the linings, buttons, and zippers. To felt the wool, wash the fabric pieces in hot water and dry on a high setting.

2 Cut and piece the scraps to create a 14×60-inch runner. Steam and press the runner. Press under ½ inch on all the raw edges.

3 Cut the teal and navy felt to measure 18×64 inches. Center the pieced runner over the teal and then the navy felt. Topstitch around the runner ⅛ inch from the folded edges.

4 Using pinking shears, cut the teal felt so it extends ¼ inch from the edge of the runner. To make the scallops, place the lid on the navy felt and trace around it. See the photograph *right* for details. Cut the scallops along the marked lines.

5 Trace leaves onto the felt, then cut out the leaves for the appliqués. Scatter the leaves along the runner. Sew them in place using one strand of tapestry yarn and a blanket stitch. Add stems using a chain stitch. To make the veins, couch matching tapestry yarn branching from the center.

place mat

1 Cut up the clothing, removing the linings, buttons, and zippers. To felt the wool, wash the fabric pieces in hot water and dry on a high setting.

2 Cut and piece the scraps to create a 14×19-inch top. Steam and press the place mat. Press under ½ inch on all the raw edges.

3 Cut the teal and navy felt to measure 18×23 inches. Center the pieced place mat over the teal and then the navy felt. Topstitch around the place mat ⅛ inch from the folded edges.

4 Using pinking shears, cut the teal felt so it extends ¼ inch from the edge of the place mat. To make the scallops, place the lid on the navy felt and trace around it. See the photograph *above* for

details. Cut the scallops along the marked lines.

5 Trace leaves onto the felt, then cut out the leaves for the appliqués. Scatter the leaves on the place mat. Sew them in place using one strand of tapestry yarn and a blanket stitch. Add stems using a chain stitch. To make the leaf veins, couch matching tapestry yarn branching from the center.

chair cover

❧ Turn the place mats into chair covers simply by adding ribbon ties. For each chair back, cut four 24-inch-long pieces of grosgrain ribbon. Machine- or hand-tack the ribbons to the backs of the place mats 3 inches down from the topstitched corners. Fold the mats over the chair backs as shown *above* and tie them in place. Trim the ribbons.

coasters

❧ Add coasters to your table setting or make sets to give as gifts. Cut 6-inch squares from the felted wool. Steam and press the wool, turning ½ inch under on the raw edges. Cut the teal and navy felt to measure 8 inches square. Assemble the coasters in the same manner as the place mats, using a quarter to create the scallop shapes around the edges. See the photographs *left* for details.

Appliqué and embroider a single leaf to each coaster, following the instructions for applying the leaves to the place mats. For interest, use a different shape and color leaf for each coaster.

fall frenzy

Wake up a sleepy room by working bold geometrics and fall colors into no-sew pillows and a decoupage lampshade.

geometric pillows

1 Cut the pillow front and back. Using modern art as your influence, draw a pattern on your paper. The image can be either cut out so the background color shows through (see the wavy pillow *bottom right*), applied to the front (see the round designs *bottom center*), or a combination (see the bar pillow *bottom left*).

2 Fuse the paper-backed web to the wrong sides of the decorative fabrics. Using a fabric marker, transfer the pattern to the decorative fabrics. Fuse the designs in place. After the fabric cools, use dots of fabric glue to tack down any loose spots.

3 On the pillow front, mark points for tying the front and back together, placing dots 2 inches in from the outer edge and spacing them 1 inch apart. Place the front over the back, wrong sides facing.

What You'll Need...

- ☐ 20-inch squares of artificial suede for the pillow front and back
- ☐ Paper for a pattern
- ☐ Assorted artificial suede scraps for the design
- ☐ Fabric glue and paper-backed fusible transfer web
- ☐ Fade-out fabric marker
- ☐ Large-eye leather needle
- ☐ Perle cotton
- ☐ 16-inch pillow form

4

5

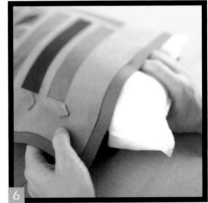

6

At each dot, thread the needle with perle cotton but do not knot the ends. Sew from front to back. Return the needle to the pillow front so two tails are left on the front. Pull the thread tightly.

Tie the perle cotton in a square knot and trim the ends. Continue sewing the pillow together on three sides, leaving the final side open.

Insert the pillow form through the opening, arranging it to fit smoothly. Tie the final side closed.

13

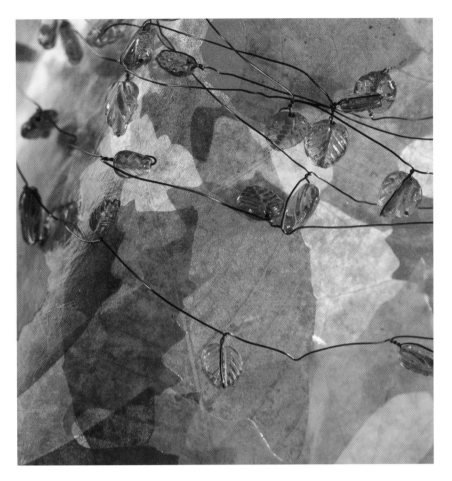

decoupage leaf lampshade

Give a plain paper lampshade the glow of autumn with paper leaves decoupaged over the surface. Paper cheese leaves are the trick. The thin, colorful leaves become transparent when the light is switched on. Overlapping the leaves adds depth to the colors.

1 Working on one side at a time, paint gloss decoupage medium onto the lampshade. Paint the back of the cheese leaves with decoupage medium and adhere the leaves to the shade. Overlap the leaves so the entire side of the shade is covered. Allow the leaves to extend beyond the upper and lower edges of the shade. Continue until the entire lampshade is covered. Cover the shade with five additional coats of decoupage medium.

2 After the decoupage medium dries, trim the leaves that extend beyond the shade top and bottom. Glue double-fold bias tape to the top and bottom edges with a hot-glue gun and glue sticks. Wrap a thin leaf garland around the shade.

What You'll Need...

- ☐ Purchased paper lampshade
- ☐ Paper cheese leaves (available at gourmet and cheese shops)
- ☐ Gloss-finish decoupage medium
- ☐ Disposable foam brush
- ☐ Double-fold bias tape
- ☐ Glue gun and glue sticks
- ☐ Wire and glass leaf garland, available at crafts and decorating stores or self-made

15

leafy looks

Bring a treetop view to your room with window treatments straight from the linens drawer. A tablecloth curtain and table runner valance both sport leaf motifs.

valance, curtain & tieback

1 Lay the runner over the sheer panel so one edge of the runner aligns with a hemmed edge of the sheer panel. Trace the outline of the valance onto the panel. Remove the valance. Cut out the sheer panel, running a hot wood-burning tool along the drawn line. The tool will cut and seal the edges simultaneously and prevent fraying. Avoid damaging your work surface by woodburning on a piece of glass, such as glass from an old picture frame.

2 Place the sheer panel over the simplest leaf patterns of the tablecloth and trace the leaves onto the panel, scattering them in a sparse but pleasing manner. Remove the tablecloth.

3

Using the wood-burning tool and referring to the photograph *above*, cut the leaf shapes from the panel.

4 Hang the tablecloth from the tension rod and clip rings, placing it inside the window frame. NOTE: If a leaf-patterned tablecloth is not available, fuse fabric leaves to a purchased curtain.

5 Glue small silk leaves over the clips of the remaining rings. Layer the panel over the table runner and hang them both from the clips. See the photographs *top* and *opposite* for details.

6 Mount the vase on the wall according to the manufacturer's instructions, placing it so it can be used as a curtain tieback. Fill the vase with fall leaves, picks, and other items. Drape the curtain over the vase. See the photographs *top right* and *opposite*.

What You'll Need...

- ☐ Purchased table runner for a valance
- ☐ Light-colored sheer polyester curtain panel
- ☐ Pencil and straightedge
- ☐ Wood-burning tool
- ☐ Glass scrap (optional)
- ☐ Purchased tablecloth with leaf designs or a plain cloth, fabric or silk leaves, and paper-backed fusible web
- ☐ Clip-style curtain rings (two sets)
- ☐ Small silk leaves or floral picks with small leaves
- ☐ Hot-glue gun and glue sticks
- ☐ Tension rod
- ☐ Hanging vase
- ☐ Various fall silk leaves, picks, and artificial gourds

▲ A Corner on Color: Give a fall classic a new shape. Cover a rectangular foam wreath form with moss. Snip leaf clusters from a silk garland or picks. Attach leaf clusters over the moss using floral pins so each cluster covers the stems and pins of the previous cluster. See the detail *above*. After the wreath front is covered, trim the leaves to accent the shape. Hang an artificial gourd from ribbon in the center.

In a Twinkling:
fall into it...

◀ Sheer Genius: Silk leaves slipped into a pocket-style place mat appear to be floating on a pond. Cut two pieces of stiff organdy 1 inch deeper than the desired finished size. Join the top edges in a French seam. Narrowly hem each bottom edge. With wrong sides facing, cut two 2½-inch-wide strips of felt; press under ½ inch along one long edge of each piece. Center and sew decorative ribbon to the felt. Slide the felt over the side edges of the place mat to encase the raw edges. Place beaded trim on the underside of the felt and pin through all layers. Topstitch the felt and beading in place along both long edges. Slip the leaves inside the place mat at the bottom open edge. The leaves can be replaced with pictures, confetti, or other flat items, depending on the season.

▼ Picture This: Customize a pillow with your own photograph or clip art. Transfer the image to a plain napkin using photo-transfer paper. Trim the napkin and center it on a larger napkin. Sew the napkins together and trim the cut edges with dried floral grass. Add another napkin for backing and sew them into a pillow.

◀ Nesting Season: Create a wall hanging or window treatment with purchased twig nests that are embellished with floral picks and leaves. Glue the trims in the nests. Glue one end of a ribbon to the underside of the nest, from the nest's center to its edge. Fold the ribbon in half and glue the remaining end over the first end, forming a large loop. Hang the nests from a curtain rod or twig.

19

▲ Bead It: Wooden curtain rings are seen in a wild new light when wrapped with beads and used as candle rings. Remove the screw eyes and paint the rings to match the beads. String beads onto 24-gauge wire. For the dangles, use leaf-shaped beads or punch your own using copper sheeting and a leaf-shaped punch. Wrap the wire around the ring at equidistant points or so most of the ring is covered. If needed, use small dots of glue on the inside of the ring to hold the beading in place.

▲ Stick 'em Up: Turn fall images into seasonal magnets with magnetized transfer paper that works in most computer printers and is available at most office supply stores. Download clip art from the Internet or software programs or scan your own photographs or actual leaves. Print the pictures onto the magnetized sheet and cut them out as shown.

Take time from the fast pace and high stress of the holidays to reflect on the true meaning of Christmas. This year, rich pastels and simple decorations make the celebration even more relaxing.

the colors of Advent

The true meaning of Advent is more than a countdown to the day Santa arrives. In the Christian church, it is a time of preparation for one of the most holy events, the celebration of the birth of Jesus Christ.

In the Christian calendar, Advent starts on the fourth Sunday before Christmas. The season is divided into four weeks, each having a separate meaning. The themes and colors have evolved throughout time and vary from church to church and family to family. Feel free to adapt the ideas shown to reflect your own beliefs and preferences.

The Advent Calendar
Our Advent calendar combines both religious and gift-giving traditions. Small pockets with ribbon trim hold trinkets or treats, and the numbered cards list Bible verses that represent each week's theme.

The Advent Wreath
A white center candle signifies Christ and is lit only on Christmas day. The four candles around it are for the four weeks of Advent. One candle is lit each week as the new theme is pondered, with the previous candles rekindled to remember their meaning. The colors may vary, but the most common are blue, purple, and pink.

The Advent Wreath

A cake pedestal forms the base for the Advent wreath shown *opposite*. Drape it with ribbons, using the candles to hold them in place. Add greens and tallow berries at the base of the candles. Change the greens often and use care when lighting the candles. Never leave lit candles unattended.

advent pockets with verses

1 Place a screw eye in each end of the dowel. Spray paint the dowel and screw eyes with two or more coats of paint.

2 For the package pockets, cut the 3-inch-wide white satin ribbon into twenty-five 3×4-inch rectangles. For the package trims, cut 25 sets of the following, cutting five sets from each color: 3½-inch, 5-inch, and 8½-inch length of ⅜-inch satin ribbon. Press under ¼ inch on the ribbon ends.

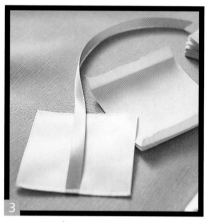

Press under ½ inch on the cut edges of each satin rectangle. These will become the pockets when sewn to the sheer ribbon. Edgestitch one folded edge for the pocket top. For each pocket, center and sew an 8½-inch ribbon on the bottom edge.

Cut five 26-inch lengths of sheer ribbon. Pin five same-color packages on each ribbon, spacing them 2¼ inches up from the bottom and leaving 1½ inches between the packages. Center a matching 3½-inch ribbon horizontally across each

package. Pin it in place. Sew one end of the 5-inch ribbon to the sheer ribbon so it is centered and the sewn edge falls just below the package top. See photograph 4 for details on all ribbon placement.

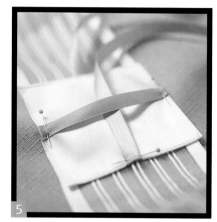

Sew the packages to the ribbon along the side and bottom edges. See photograph 5 for details. Arrange the sheer ribbons on the dowel, leaving about 1½ inches between the rows. Hot-glue the top edge of the ribbons to the back of the dowel. Trim the free ends into an inverted V shape. To hang the dowel, run the remaining ⅜-inch ribbons through the screw eyes, leaving long tails at the sides. Knot the ribbons around the screw eyes and trim the tails.

6 To make the scripture cards, cut twenty-five 1½×3-inch rectangles from card stock. Fold the rectangles in half crosswise. Adhere or write the numbers 1–25 on the card fronts. On the card backs, cut two ½-inch-long horizontal slits. Center the lower slit both horizontally and vertically. Place the second slit ¼ inch directly over the first slit.

What You'll Need...

- [ ] 21-inch length of ½-inch-diameter dowel
- [ ] Two ⅜-inch screw eyes
- [ ] White spray paint
- [ ] 3 yards of 3-inch-wide white satin ribbon
- [ ] 4 yards each of five pastel colors of ⅜-inch-wide satin ribbon
- [ ] 4 yards of 3-inch-wide wire-edged white sheer ribbon
- [ ] Hot-glue gun and glue sticks
- [ ] White card stock
- [ ] 1 sheet each of papers to match the five pastel ribbons
- [ ] Number stickers or permanent marker
- [ ] Crafts knife
- [ ] Black fine-tipped permanent marker
- [ ] Crafts glue
- [ ] Small gifts for the pockets

Cut each of the pastel papers into five 1¼×2¾-inch rectangles. Fold the rectangles in half crosswise. Write a scripture verse on the inside. To attach a card to each package, weave the 8½-inch ribbon through the slits. Slide the card down the ribbon. See photograph 7 for details. Glue the pastel card to the numbered card on the inside; do not glue over the slits.

8 Place a small gift in each pocket. Tie the top and bottom ribbons in a bow. See the photograph on *page 20* for details.

22

Hope

Week One: HOPE AND ANTICIPATION

Suggested Bible Verses: *Psalms 37:9; Psalms 40:1; Psalms 62:5; Isaiah 40:31; Isaiah 52:7–10; Jeremiah 29:11–13; Matthew 1:1–11; Romans 8:18–27; Romans 12:9–21; Romans 15:4; 1 Corinthians 13:13; 1 Thessalonians 1:2–10; 1 Timothy 4:10; Hebrews 10:19–25; Hebrews 11:1*

Love

Week Two: LOVE AND KINDNESS

Suggested Bible Verses: *John 13:34–35; Romans 13:8–14; 1 Corinthians 1; Ephesians 3:14–21; 1 John 3:1–3; 1 John 3:6–20; 1 John 4:7–12*

23

Joy

Week Three: JOY AND CELEBRATION

Suggested Bible Verses: *Psalms 51:10–12; Psalms 71:19–24; Matthew 2:9–11; Matthew 13:44–46; Luke 1:39–45; Luke 2:8–12; Philippians 4:4; Philemon 4–7; 1 Peter 1:8–9*

Peace

Week Four: PEACE AND HARMONY

Suggested Bible Verses: *Isaiah 9:6–7; Isaiah 26:3; Isaiah 53:1–6; Matthew 14:22–33; John 14:23–27; John 16:33; John 20:19–20; Romans 15:13; Ephesians 6:10–20; Philippians 4:6–7*

24

What You'll Need...

- [ ] 1 sheet ivory-colored embossed paper
- [ ] Tacky crafts glue
- [ ] 1½-inch plastic foam cube
- [ ] 5-inch piece of ⅜-inch-diameter dowel
- [ ] 5×1¼-inch piece of red print paper
- [ ] 1¼ yards of 1-inch-wide sheer ribbon with a silver or white edge
- [ ] Sewing needle
- [ ] Red thread
- [ ] 9 inches of narrow red cording
- [ ] Straight pins

Red and white spell pure delight on a bright but sophisticated tree. Pinecones with giant ribbon scales, a ruffled topiary, a satin ornament with pleated trim, and an origami-style rosette make bold statements against the green boughs. The handmade decorations are highlighted by white lights, red and white balls in satin and shiny finishes, and deeply swagged strands of bead garland. To make your work easy, use the best-quality ribbons you can afford and avoid those that are stiff, show wrinkles, or keep permanent crease lines.

topiary ornament

1 Cut the topiary base from the ivory paper following the pattern on *page 157*. Fold the topiary base as directed on the pattern and glue it together. Cut the plastic foam to fit inside the topiary base and glue it in place. Cover the top with a scrap of ivory paper.

2 Taper one end of the dowel into a point using a pencil sharpener. Glue the red paper over the dowel, twisting it to a point at the sharpened end. Glue the flat end of the dowel into the center of the topiary base, pushing it into the foam as far as possible.

3 Hand-sew a row of gathering stitches along one long edge of the sheer ribbon. Taper each end to a point as you gather. Pull up the gather so the ribbon measures 8½ inches and knot, but do not cut the thread. Adjust the gathers so they are even.

4 Starting at the end with the needle still attached, wrap the end of the ribbon around the dowel point once. Sew the ribbon in place, stitching through the paper point. Spiral the ribbon around the dowel, ending with a complete ruffle at top of the base. Pin the ruffle to the plastic foam. Sew a narrow cord to the top ruffle for a hanger.

25

seeing red

Red ribbons look pretty on the bolt, but when pleated, twirled, folded, and tucked, they turn into spectacular tree trims. White fabrics, papers, and beading set off their color in a crisp way.

- ☐ 3⁷/₈×2⁷/₈-inch plastic foam egg
- ☐ 6-inch square and 2-inch circle of ivory fabric
- ☐ 3¼ yards of ⁵/₈-inch-wide double-faced satin ribbon
- ☐ 1 yard of ½-inch-wide red seam binding
- ☐ Beads in the following sizes and colors: size 11/0 red seed beads, 4-mm silver rounds, 4-mm red rounds, 6-mm red rounds
- ☐ Straight pins
- ☐ Beading needle
- ☐ ¾-inch-diameter wooden wheel
- ☐ 9 inches 4-mm silk ribbon
- ☐ Large-eye embroidery needle
- ☐ Red thread

ribbon pinecone

1 Pin the center of the fabric square to the tip of the egg. Stretch and pin the fabric over the egg. The egg will not be entirely covered. Measure 2½ inches up from the tip of the egg and mark all around the egg.

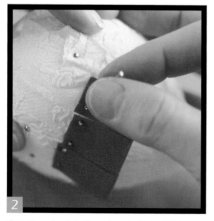

2

Cut the double-faced satin into 58 two-inch-long pieces. Working with one piece at a time, fold it in half so the cut edges meet. Pin the cut edges to the egg along the marked line. See the photograph *above* for details. Repeat with 13 more loops, placing them close together. Pin bias tape over the cut edges.

3 Pin a second layer of 15 loops ½ inch above the folded edge of the first row. Cover the cut edges with bias tape. Repeat this pattern using the following number of loops: row three, 15 loops; row four, 14 loops.

4 For the final row, cut twelve 3-inch strips of bias tape. Fold one strip into a loop. Using a double thread, run a gathering stitch ¼ inch from the cut edge. Do not cut the thread. Repeat with the remaining loops until you have a chain of 12 loops. Pull the thread so the loops gather as tightly as possible. Tack the first loop to the last one and knot the thread. Trim the seam allowance to ⅛ inch. Pin the gathered ring to the top of the egg, adjusting it as you pin.

5 Bead the loops and the pinecone bottom as shown *above left* or as desired. Beginning ½ inch below the bottom folded edge, pin seven vertical rows of red seed beads to the white portion of the pinecone.

6 Cover the wheel with the remaining fabric. Slip both ends of the 4mm silk ribbon through an embroidery needle eye and pierce through the center of the wheel. Knot the ribbon ends on the underside and pin the knot to the center top of the pinecone. Slip the wheel down to the pinecone and glue it in place. Slide a 6mm red bead over the loop and down to the wheel.

rosette ornament

1 Using the pattern on *page 156*, cut two small octagons from cardboard. Cut two large octagons from fabric, using the pattern. Mark each center. Press under ½ inch on the raw edges of both fabric pieces.

26

What You'll Need...

- ☐ 8×16-inch piece of red raw silk or similar fabric
- ☐ 4X8-inch piece of lightweight cardboard or poster board
- ☐ Red thread
- ☐ Two 6mm silver beads
- ☐ 7 flat red teardrop beads
- ☐ Seven 4-mm round silver beads
- ☐ Seven 6-mm round red beads
- ☐ Four 4-mm round red beads
- ☐ Silver seed beads

2 Place one fabric octagon wrong-side up. Center a cardboard octagon over the fabric. Using a doubled thread, stitch through the center of the fabric and cardboard. Do not cut the thread.

3 Fold one flat edge up to the center of the octagon. Tack the center of that side to the center of the octagon, sewing through all layers of the fabric and the cardboard. Rotate the fabric and repeat folding and stitching at the next flat side. See photograph 3 for details. Repeat until all the flat edges are folded up. Press the folds. Repeat with the second octagon. Sew a 6mm silver bead to the center of each octagon.

4 Place the two octagons together, flat sides facing. Tack each point. Make seven bead strands in the following pattern: red teardrop, 4-mm round silver, 6mm round red. Stitch a bead dangle to all but the top point. See the photograph *opposite* for details. Make a hanging loop of silver seed beads and 4-mm red beads and tack it to the remaining top point.

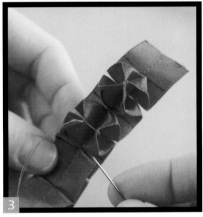

What You'll Need...

- ☐ Purchased red satin ornament
- ☐ 1-inch-wide double-faced satin ribbon to match the ornament (see instructions to calculate length measurement)
- ☐ Fade-out fabric marker
- ☐ Sewing pins
- ☐ Red thread
- ☐ Silver seed beads
- ☐ 4 bugle beads
- ☐ Four 6-mm gray pearls

box-pleated satin ornament

1 To determine the length of ribbon needed for the band, measure around the ornament where the pleating will be placed. Triple this measurement and add 1 inch for overlap.

2 Beginning 1/2 inch from one end, measure and mark the ribbon at 3/4-inch intervals. Using the marks as guides, pleat the ribbon according to the diagram *below*. Hold the pleats in place with pins until the entire ribbon is pleated. Lightly press the pleats, then machine-stitch down the center of the ribbon parallel to the selvage edges. Remove the pins and press the pleats in place.

3 Fold the ribbon right sides together along the stitching line and press. If desired, tack the selvage edges together at the center of each wide pleat. See photograph 3 for details.

4 Wrap the ribbon around the ornament and pin it in place. These pins will be removed later. Turn under one raw edge and overlap the other raw edge. Slip a silver seed bead onto a pin and pin the ends in place. Place additional seed beads and pins between each box pleat. See the photograph *above* for details. Remove the first set of pins, leaving only the beaded pins.

5 Make four beaded dangles in the following pattern: seed bead, bugle bead, seed bead, 6-mm pearl, seed bead. Stitch the dangles to the ribbon at equal intervals.

27

Any climate can inspire a white Christmas. In this home, starfish and seashells replace snowflakes and icicles for a holiday look that rolls with good "tide-ings."

a seaside Christmas

Who would guess that a house filled with seashells and other beach findings isn't close to the shore? You'll find this tribute to the coast in the cold, snowy upper Midwest. Seashells, starfish, and sand dollars collected on family vacations are fond reminders of quality time spent together. Add souvenirs donated by family and friends and shells purchased at crafts stores or beachside shops and soon the home is brimming with warm reminders of favorite people and places.

On the tree, *opposite*, a pair of giant starfish acts as natural toppers. Shells cut into lacy shapes, others in their natural state, and angels made from clam shells complement the seaside motif. Mirrored balls, shiny silver and white ornaments, and hundreds of white lights add a luminous glow. Yard after yard of pearlescent and crystal garland add the finishing touch.

More beach combings line the mantel *opposite* and on *page 30*. Adding candles and a mirror reflects the elegant look, giving it even more impact.

In the dining room on *page 31*, seashells form an impromptu mobile when dangled from a wreath-wrapped chandelier. Seeded eucalyptus misted with silver paint forms the chandelier wreath. On the table, a ring of misted seed sprigs is pinned to the table covering to frame the dessert buffet. Ornaments, sand dollars, and starfish dance in the sun that shines as brightly on the snowy scene beyond the windows as it does on the beach.

starfish ornament

 To hang the starfish, carefully drill a 1/16-inch hole in one leg of the starfish. Run a strand of monofilament through the hole for a hanging loop.

What You'll Need...

- [ ] Seeded eucalyptus
- [ ] Silver floral spray
- [ ] Wire wreath form large enough to fit around the chandelier base
- [ ] Paddle-style floral wire
- [ ] Heavy wire for hanging the wreath
- [ ] Ribbon to cover the wires
- [ ] Monofilament
- [ ] Shells and ornaments

chandelier mobile

1 Lightly mist the eucalyptus with floral spray, giving it a slight shimmer. Snip the eucalyptus into sprigs, then group the sprigs into clusters. Using paddle wire, attach the clusters to the wreath form. Add more sprigs, using each to cover the stems and wires of the previous bundles. Do not cut the wire; use it in one continuous strand. Continue until the wreath form is covered and full.

2 Firmly attach heavier wires to the wreath form at four equidistant points. Have one person hold the wreath level and even with the chandelier base. Have a second person attach the wires to the top of the chandelier. Make sure the wreath is secure. Cover the hanging wires with ribbons.

3 Tie seashells, ornaments, and starfish to monofilament. Tie the monofilament to the wreath so the decorative items hang at different lengths and resemble a mobile.

seashell candlelight

What You'll Need...

- [ ] Large clear glass footed hurricanes, compotes, or other containers
- [ ] White pillar candles
- [ ] Floral tape or candle tack
- [ ] Seashells

Make even the plainest seashells twinkle by placing them in clear crystal hurricanes and adding chunky pillar candles. Choose a variety of hurricanes, compotes, and other large, deep clear glass containers. Place a white pillar candle in most of the containers. If the candle does not sit securely, add floral adhesive or candle tack to the bottom or rim of the candle. Carefully add seashells around the candles. Place small shells so they are about one-third to one-half of the way up the candle. Starfish, sand dollars, and other large shells can sit higher as long as they stay well away from the flames. To best show the shapes of the shells, use only one type of shell per container. Scatter more shells along the mantel or table and add a few bowls or containers that do not contain candles. Never leave burning candles unattended.

sweet thoughts

Yipes, stripes! These giant pop-art candy cane and peppermint stick pillows bring a festive attitude to any room.

candy cane pillows

1 For the large or small candy cane pillow, enlarge the pattern on *page 155* to full size. Place the pattern on the bias of the fabric so the stripes are diagonal. Cut out the candy cane. Repeat for the back side, matching the stripes and reversing the pattern.

2 With right sides facing, sew the pieces together along the long seams. On the curled end of the cane, re-fold the ends so the seams match and sew the ends closed. Leave the bottom open. Trim the seams, clip the curves, and turn right sides out.

3 Firmly stuff the candy cane with fiberfill. Fold the open ends so the seams match, turning in the raw edges. Blindstitch the opening closed.

peppermint stick pillow

1 For the peppermint stick bolster pillow, cut a 21×32-inch rectangle of fabric with the stripes on the bias. Fold the fabric lengthwise with right sides facing. Sew along the long edge.

2 On one short end, turn the tube so the seams match. Sew across the end. Leave the other end open. Trim the seams, clip the corners, and turn right sides out.

3 Firmly stuff the pillow with fiberfill. Fold the open end so the seams match, turning in the raw edges. Blindstitch the opening closed.

33

What You'll Need...

- ☐ 1 yard of red-and-white striped medium-weight fabric for each pillow
- ☐ Paper for a pattern
- ☐ Polyester fiberfill

beauty afoot

Pack those stockings with personality by using fun combinations of novel fabrics and trims.

What You'll Need...

- ☐ 1 yard of ivory boiled wool, wool felt, or polar fleece for the stocking
- ☐ ⅓ yard of tan boiled wool, wool felt, or polar fleece for the cuff
- ☐ Fade-away fabric marker
- ☐ 20 No. 3 safety pins
- ☐ 20 fender washers, size 1x¼ inch
- ☐ 20 silver pony beads
- ☐ 18 inches of small-link nickel-finish chain
- ☐ 3 yards 2-inch-wide silver wire-edge ribbon

4

To make the jingle trim, slide a washer and then a bead onto a pin. Working from the front, push the pin through the fabric at the dots and close it on the underneath side. See the photograph *above* for details. Hand-tack a chain end to each side seam on the inside. Tie the ribbon in a bow and tack it to the edge of the stocking as shown *opposite*.

What You'll Need...

- ☐ ⅓ yard of ivory boiled wool, wool felt, or polar fleece for each triangle
- ☐ 8x18-inch piece of stiffened felt
- ☐ fade-away fabric marker
- ☐ 13 No. 3 safety pins
- ☐ 13 fender washers, size 1x¼ inch
- ☐ 13 silver pony beads

35

white jingle stocking

1 For the stocking, enlarge the pattern on *page 157*. Cut one front and one back from the ivory fabric. Cut a 19x6-inch cuff from tan. With right sides facing and using ½-inch seams, sew the stocking front to the back. Do not sew the top edges. Clip the curves, turn the stocking to the right side, and press.

2 Mark the lower edge of the cuff for the placement of the pins. Place a dot every ¾ inch, 1 inch up from the edge. Sew the short ends of the cuff together, right sides facing. Turn and press.

3 Slip the cuff over the stocking with the wrong side of the cuff facing the right side of the stocking. Turn 1½ inches of the cuff to the inside of the stocking and sew it in place.

mantel scarf

1 To make the mantel scarf, determine how many triangles will be needed. Each triangle is a separate piece that measures 15 inches across at the top. The triangles can be overlapped as much as desired.

2 Enlarge the pattern on *page 157* and cut out the triangles. Starting at the lower point, mark the pin placement every 1½ inches, 1 inch from the edge.

3

Lay the stiffened felt over the triangle along placement line and topstitch the felt in place. This will lie along the mantel top, allowing the triangles to hang down. See photograph 3 and *opposite* for details.

4 Make and attach the jingle trim as described in step 4 for the stocking. See photograph 3 for details.

vintage linens stockings

1 Enlarge the stocking pattern on *page 157*. Lay the pattern over the poster board and trace around the pattern. Cut along the line and remove the stocking shape to make a stencil. Using a stencil instead of a pattern will help make the best use of the fabric's design and avoid any flaws.

2 Move the stencil over the stocking fabric to find the best of the fabric's pattern. Concentrate most of the design on the lower part of the stocking. *Note:* The stocking does not need to be cut on the fabric's straight grain. When you have found the best design, trace along the inside of the stencil.

3 Fuse interfacing to the wrong side of the fabric under and beyond the design area. Cut out the stocking front, adding ⅝-inch seam allowances. Repeat for the stocking back.

4 Sew the stocking front to the back, right sides facing. Leave the top edge open. Clip and trim the seams. Turn the stocking to the right side and press.

5 Prepare the lining in the same manner as the stocking but do not turn. Slide the lining into the stocking, wrong sides facing. Smooth out the stocking and baste the top edges together.

6 For the crochet cuff, turn the upper 1 inch of the stocking to the inside and topstitch. Cut a piece of vintage crochet trim to fit around the stocking top, allowing for ¼-inch seams at the ends. Sew the short edges together, zigzagging the seam allowances to prevent fraying. Blindstitch the trim to the stocking top.

7 For the stocking cuffs, cut a 25x5-inch strip from coordinating fabric. Sew the short ends together, adjusting the

What You'll Need...

- Vintage linens such as tablecloths, mantel cloths, or bedspreads for the stocking
- Large poster board
- Crafts knife
- Fade-away fabric marker
- 2 yards of fusible interfacing
- 1 yard of white muslin for the lining
- Coordinating vintage fabric or crochet trim for the cuff
- 2½ yards of 4-inch-wide wire-edged ribbon

size as needed. Hem the lower edge. Slide the cuff inside the stocking, matching the seams and with the right side of the cuff facing the wrong side of the stocking. Sew around the top edge. Fold the cuff to the outside, encasing the raw edges.

8 If desired, cut a hanging loop from fabric scraps. Hem the edges and sew it to the corner. Tie the ribbon in a bow and tack it in place.

36

What You'll Need...

- ☐ 18-inch-diameter purchased wreath
- ☐ Oranges, tangerines, kumquats, and walnuts
- ☐ Cinnamon sticks
- ☐ Small wired gold ball cluster ornaments
- ☐ Silk florist's leaves
- ☐ Metallic gold spray paint
- ☐ Floral wire
- ☐ Wire cutters
- ☐ Drill and small bit
- ☐ 1-inch-diameter gold jingle bells
- ☐ Spray flocking
- ☐ 1½ yards of ribbon for the bow

wreaths that welcome

frosted fruit

1 Prepare the elements. Slice the oranges thinly and bake in a 250°F oven until dry. Thread a wire through each slice and twist to secure. Thread wire up one tube of each cinnamon stick and back down through the other tube. Place two cinnamon sticks together and twist the wires tightly. Spray the leaves gold. When the leaves dry, twist three leaves around the stems of the ball clusters. Drill holes through the wide end of the walnuts. Insert wires and twist them. Push a wire through each orange and tangerine. Join trios of kumquats together with wire. See the photograph *above* for details.

2 Flock the wreath according to the manufacturer's directions and let it dry. To create the fruit sprays, wire the oranges and tangerines to one section of the wreath. Add the kumquat and gold ball clusters. Fill in with orange slices, bells, cinnamon sticks, and nuts.

3 Add a bow. Lightly spray the entire wreath with flocking.

Christmas carol

1 Spray paint the following items: fern stems, calla lilies, magnolia leaves, and pinecones. Separate the ivy picks and bead spray. Cut the paper into leaf or star shapes and crumple it, then smooth it out.

2 Wire the calla lilies and magnolia leaves to the lower right side of the wreath. Add the remaining items in the order listed, spacing them in a pleasing manner and using wire to hold them in place.

39

What You'll Need...

- ☐ 18-inch-diameter purchased wreath
- ☐ Gold metallic spray paint
- ☐ Fern stems, calla lilies, magnolia leaves, and small pinecones
- ☐ Ecru-colored ivy picks
- ☐ Gold-flecked bead spray
- ☐ Decorative paper with handwriting or music notes
- ☐ Assorted 3- to 5-inch gold-colored musical instruments
- ☐ Floral wire
- ☐ Floral tape
- ☐ Wire cutters

Take one ordinary purchased wreath, add gatherings from the crafts store, produce aisle, or your collections, and you have a custom-made wreath that matches your home's personality.

candy striper

1 Cut the ribbon in half. Pin and sew the two lengths together along the long edges. See the photograph *right*.

What You'll Need...

☐ 18-inch-diameter purchased wreath
☐ 4 yards of 2- to 3-inch-wide red-and-white striped grosgrain ribbon
☐ Pins

2 To make the bow, cut a 36-inch length of the joined ribbon. Hem both ends. Starting at the left, measure out 25 inches. Fold the ribbon back on itself 10 inches. Sew the end to the ribbon to secure the loop. Place your fingers in the fold. Open out the loop and bring the fold to the seamline. Tack it in place, forming the lower loop that also measures 10 inches. Place your fingers on the left fold. Open out the loop and bring the fold to the seamline. This forms the top loop.

3 Fold the remaining ribbon in half for the tails. Tack the bow over the tails. Place the bow on the side of the wreath. Wrap the free end of the ribbon around the greens and secure it with pins.

41

western wonder

1 To make the bandanna balls, stretch the bandanna fabric tightly over the plastic foam balls, making the best use of the printed design. Twist the excess fabric together, secure it with wire and pins, and trim away as much as possible. See the photograph *left* for details.

2 Wrap the belt around the wreath, buckle it, and arrange it among the greens. Run wire through the bandanna balls and attach them to the wreath around the belt. Add the small ornaments for sparkle.

What You'll Need...

- [ ] 18-inch-diameter purchased wreath
- [ ] Bandannas
- [ ] 3-inch-diameter plastic foam balls
- [ ] Straight pins
- [ ] Floral wire
- [ ] Wire cutters
- [ ] Inexpensive beaded belt
- [ ] 1-inch-diameter balls

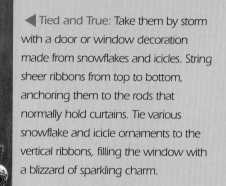

Tied and True: Take them by storm with a door or window decoration made from snowflakes and icicles. String sheer ribbons from top to bottom, anchoring them to the rods that normally hold curtains. Tie various snowflake and icicle ornaments to the vertical ribbons, filling the window with a blizzard of sparkling charm.

In a Twinkling:
decorations

Gilded Treasure: Miniature wreaths made of golden leaves anchor holiday candles, turning them into an elegant arrangement. Starting about ¾ inch from the base of a green silk leaf, twist the stem of that leaf to the stem of a second leaf. Repeat, using 12 leaves and shaping them into a circle. Using gold metallic paint, spray both sides of the wreath with two or more coats.

▶ Now Starring: There's no rule that says a wreath has to be full and fluffy. This shining example has charm in its simplicity. Bend wire into a star shape for the frame. (It doesn't have to be perfect.) Using floral wire, attach boxwood sprigs to the frame. Top it with an organza bow, then dangle a sparkling star in the center.

◀ Urned Style: Take holiday decorating to new heights by lining a cupboard top with a row of tiny silk trees nestled in urns. Weave tallow berry garland around the urns for a bright but lacy look.

43

◀ The Written Word: Spell out your own holiday wishes on a hand-lettered pillow. Type out various greetings on a computer using different fonts or enlarge the pattern on *page 156.* Lay lightweight cotton fabric over the words and trace them using red and green permanent fabric marking pens. Assemble the fabric into a pillow or pillow cover, adding trims such as bows and bells.

sitting pretty

Gussy up your chairs for the holidays in the most novel ways. Unexpected materials such as place mats, table runners, pillowcases, and even winter scarves and mittens make everyone sit up and take notice.

snowflake slip

What You'll Need...

- ☐ 100-percent-cotton pillowcase
- ☐ Poster board
- ☐ Acrylic paints and textile medium
- ☐ Rubber stamps with snowflake designs
- ☐ Disposable foam paintbrush
- ☐ Snowflake garland and ornaments

1 Wash and dry the pillowcase. Do not use fabric softener, dryer sheets, or detergents with additives. Iron the case, making sure to crease the fold opposite the seam on the long side. (The crease marks the slit position.) Slip the case over the chair back and mark the seat position at the sides of the case. Remove the case and slit it open to the marks. Narrowly hem the slits. See photograph 3 for how the slits look on the finished slipcover.

2 Cut the poster board to fit inside the case and slide it in place. Mix the paints with textile medium according to the package instructions. Lightly paint one of the rubber stamps. See photograph 2 for details. Press the stamp onto the case. Repeat with additional stamps and colors until one side is covered. Clean the stamps before switching colors. Let the paint dry and repeat on the other side. Heat-set the paint according to the manufacturer's instructions.

3 Tack the snowflake garland to the bottom edge of what will be the back side of the slipcover. Place the cover over the chair so the flap hangs down in the back and lies flat across the seat in the front. See photograph 3 for details.

4 To shape the upper corners of the slipcover around the chair top, fold the corners to the back. Tack a snowflake ornament to each point for weight.

What You'll Need...

- [ ] Heavy place mat with fringed ends
- [ ] 2 yards of contrasting narrow cording
- [ ] 2 large buttons
- [ ] ⅓ yard of matching ⅜-inch-wide ribbon

place mat top

1 Fold the place mat in half over the chair back so the fringe hangs down. Mark spots on either side under the top rail where the buttons will be placed. See the second chair from the left for details of the button placement.

2 Cut three graduated lengths of cording. Drape the cording across the place mat with the ends of the cording at the marked spots. Zigzag over the ends. Sew a button over the cording ends to cover the stitching.

3 Fit the folded place mat to the chair back. Cut the ribbon in half. Shape each piece into a loop. Pin each loop to the wrong side of the front half of the topper. Adjust the loops so they slip around the buttons, connecting the topper front to the topper back, holding it in place. Remove the topper and hand-sew the ribbon ends. Slip it over the chair and button in place.

What You'll Need...

☐ Purchased table runner with decorative ends
☐ Self-adhesive hook-and-loop dots

runner drape

1 Lay the table runner evenly over the chair back. Pull both ends to the back of the chair so none of the runner falls onto the chair seat.

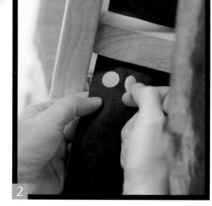

2 Lift the back of the table runner and apply the hook-and-loop dots to the wrong side of each panel just under the lowest rung of the chair back. This will keep the runner from sliding. NOTE: For an elegant look, use a long runner with tassels and allow the tassels to drape onto the floor.

What You'll Need...

☐ Large holiday dish towel
☐ 25 to 30 silver jingle bells in assorted sizes
☐ Narrow silver cording
☐ Large-eye tapestry needle
☐ Wide ribbon

towel cover-up

Using a loose whipstitch, sew the bells to the bottom of one end of a dish towel. To whipstitch, insert the threaded needle from the back to the front. Slide a bell onto the cording and bring the needle down through the front of the towel. Leave the cord loose so the bell dangles slightly. Continue across the towel, letting the bells hang at different lengths. See photograph 1.

2 Drape the towel over the chair back, gathering it to fit within the outer upright rungs of the back. Adjust the towel so the hem of the towel meets the seat at the front of the chair and hangs longer in the back.

3 Cinch the towel slightly and tie it in place with ribbon using either a bow or knot. Adjust the gathers.

What You'll Need...

☐ Winter scarves, small mittens or gloves, and knit ski-style headbands in coordinating colors
☐ Safety pins, corsage pins, or T-pins

muffler back

1 Layer and wrap the scarves around the back of the chair. Pull the ends from front to back so none of the fabric rests on the chair seat.

Gather up the scarves with the headbands, wrapping them around the scarves several times. Twist the headbands to display the different colors.

3 Tuck the mittens or gloves into the headbands as shown in photograph 2, fanning them to create a focal point. If necessary, pin the different elements in place to keep them from shifting.

purely ornamental

foiled

What You'll Need...

- ☐ Matte-finish, frosted white ball ornament
- ☐ Pencil
- ☐ 1/8-inch double-sided tacky crafts tape
- ☐ Medium-weight silver metal sheet
- ☐ Decorative-edge scissors

1 Mark eight equidistant lines around the ball from top to bottom. Run 1/8-inch-wide tape along these lines. Do not remove the paper backing.

2 Cut the metal into eight 3/16-inch-wide strips that reach from cap to bottom. Narrowly trim half the strips with decorative-edge scissors. Remove the paper backing from the tape and press the metal to the tape, alternating straight and shaped stripes.

What You'll Need...

- ☐ Matte-finish, frosted white ball ornament
- ☐ Medium-weight silver metal sheet
- ☐ Stylus or sharpened pencil with an eraser
- ☐ 4-mm rhinestones
- ☐ Adhesive for glass and other slick surfaces

Turn plain matte-finish white balls into little works of art by adding silver trims. When placed on an all-white tree, the look is understated and elegant.

foiled again

1 Draw simple flower shapes onto the metal and cut them out. Lay the flowers right side down on a soft surface. Using the stylus or the pencil eraser, shape the petals. Turn the flower over and use the stylus or pencil to make an indentation in the center.

2 Glue a rhinestone to the center of the flower. Glue several flowers to the ball, gently shaping them.

What You'll Need...

- ☐ Matte-finish, frosted white ball ornament
- ☐ Pencil
- ☐ ¼-inch double-sided tacky crafts tape
- ☐ Shallow container
- ☐ Tiny silver glass marbles

beaded strands

1 Cut strips of ¼-inch tape to fit around the ball from top to bottom at equidistant points. Leaving the paper on the outer side of the tape, press the tape to the ball. NOTE: The tape also can be applied horizontally or spiraled around the ball.

2 Pour the marbles into a shallow container. Remove the paper backing from the tape and press the taped sections into the container so the tape becomes covered with silver marbles. Use your fingers to add marbles to any sparse spots, then firmly press the marbles into the tape.

■ Basic crafting supplies are all it takes to make these elegant silver and white ornaments. In addition to the tape, glitter, metal, brushes, leafing, eyelets, pearls, marbles, and punches listed, consider using glitter slivers and silver paint pens.

3 Dilute the glue with water so it is thin enough to apply with the liner brush. Paint thin stripes of glue onto the ball, centering them on the stripes.

4 While the glue is wet, pour glitter over the ball, letting the excess fall onto the paper plate. Repeat if needed.

What You'll Need...

- ☐ Matte-finish, frosted white ball ornament
- ☐ ⅛- and ⅜-inch double-sided tacky crafts tape
- ☐ Medium-weight silver metal sheet
- ☐ Fine silver glitter
- ☐ Small star punch

51

stars in stripes

1 From the ⅛-inch and ⅜-inch crafts tape, cut four lengths each; cut each long enough to reach from the top of the ball to the bottom. Do not remove the paper backing. Press the tape to the ball at equidistant intervals. Alternate between wide and narrow tape.

2 Pour the glitter into a shallow container. Remove the paper backing from the narrow stripes and press the tape into the glitter.

3 Cut ½-inch-wide strips of metal to fit over the wider tape. Punch star shapes down the center of the strips. Remove the paper backing from the tape and press the foil to the tape.

4 Roll the ball in the glitter to cover the star openings in the metal stripes.

What You'll Need...

- ☐ Matte-finish, frosted white ball ornament
- ☐ ³⁄₁₆-inch-diameter star-shape eyelets
- ☐ Adhesive for glass and other slick surfaces
- ☐ 4-mm pearls

What You'll Need...

- ☐ Matte-finish, frosted white ball ornament
- ☐ Silver leafing kit
- ☐ ¼-inch flat brush and liner brush
- ☐ Tacky glue
- ☐ Paper plate
- ☐ Fine silver glitter

stars in their eyelets

1 Apply glue to the flat side of the eyelet. Press the eyelet to the ornament. Let the glue dry. Repeat, adding eyelets all around the ball.

2 Glue a pearl to the center of each eyelet. Let the glue dry.

leaf it simple

1 Using the flat brush, paint leafing adhesive onto the ball according to the manufacturer's instructions. Let the adhesive dry. The ball shown *opposite right* has concentric stripes, but any other simple pattern may be used.

2 Lay a sheet of silver leaf over the adhesive. For ease, work in small sections. Rub the leaf into the adhesive with your fingers. Remove the paper or tissue backing, leaving the silver pattern. Repeat for the next section and fill in any remaining bare spots.

folk art fellows

Add color to a wintry window scene or merriment to a mantel with this tall, twiggy Santa and Rudolph.

santa

1 Using the patterns on *page 156,* cut the suit and hat from red. On the suit, mark the fold line on the wrong side and cut the slit as marked Cut the hat band from ivory, using pinking shears on one long edge. Use pinking shears to cut an ivory beard.

2 Cut pairs of twigs as follows: 4½ inches for arms; 6 to 7 inches for legs; two 1½ inches for neck pieces. Using large dollops of hot glue, attach the arms, legs, and neck pieces to a 2-inch-square cardboard body as shown in the photograph *above.*

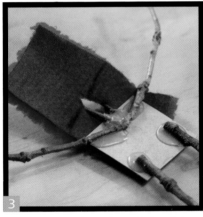

3
Slide the neck pieces through the slit in the suit as shown in photo 3.

4
Fold the suit along the fold line and glue it in place as shown in photo 4. The neck pieces should extend beyond the slit in the suit.

What You'll Need...

- ☐ Twigs
- ☐ Pruners
- ☐ Lightweight cardboard
- ☐ Red plush or boiled wool
- ☐ Ivory felt or boiled wool
- ☐ Pinking shears
- ☐ Glue gun and glue sticks
- ☐ Twine or cord for the belt
- ☐ Small wooden star
- ☐ White acrylic paint
- ☐ Small paint brush
- ☐ Multicolor glitter
- ☐ Silk evergreen sprig
- ☐ Scraps of tan polar fleece
- ☐ Red bead for the reindeer nose
- ☐ Yellow-green stiffened felt
- ☐ Thick green wool or felt

5 Glue the hat to the top of the neck twigs and glue the band over the hat as shown *opposite.* Glue the beard in place. Tack the belt over the suit.

6 Paint the star white. While the paint is still wet, sprinkle it with glitter. Trim the evergreen sprig into a tree shape. Brush the tips with white paint. Glue the star over the belt and the tree to one hand.

reindeer

1 Following the pattern on *page 156,* cut two reindeer bodies from cardboard. Glue the bodies to the wrong side of the tan felt with one facing left and one facing right. Trim the felt, leaving ½ inch beyond the cardboard. Turn the excess to the back side of the cardboard and glue it down.

2 Cut four 5-inch-long twigs for the legs and a 2-inch-long branching twig for the antlers. Cut two ears from tan and one tail from ivory. Pleat the ears at the bottom edge and glue. Fringe the curved edge of the tail.

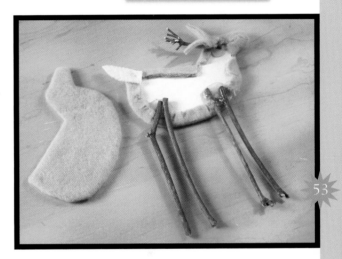

53

3 Glue the legs, tail, and one ear to a body piece as shown *above.* Add twig antlers and the second ear. Glue the second body over the first, sandwiching the legs, ears, antlers, and tail between them. Glue the nose in place.

trees

1 Cut long, narrow triangles from the stiffened felt for the tree shapes. Glue twigs in place for the trunks.

2 Glue the trees to the green fabric, wrong sides facing. Trim away the excess green material so the layers match.

NOTE: All the figures can be hung from monofilament if desired.

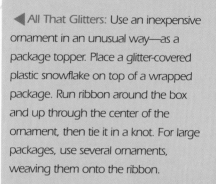

All That Glitters: Use an inexpensive ornament in an unusual way—as a package topper. Place a glitter-covered plastic snowflake on top of a wrapped package. Run ribbon around the box and up through the center of the ornament, then tie it in a knot. For large packages, use several ornaments, weaving them onto the ribbon.

In a Twinkling:

ornaments

Tiny Treasure: A baby spoon, souvenir, or other collectible spoon becomes a sparkling ornament. Drill tiny holes in the top of the handle and the tip of the bowl. Thread ribbon through the handle. Slide beads onto the ribbon. Knot the ribbon, add a vintage button, and knot the ribbon again. Tie the ends into a loop. Place more beads, including a teardrop, onto a head pin and attach them to the hole in the bowl.

▶ A Pretty Pair: Take inspiration from expensive dangling ornaments in high-end boutiques and antiques shops. Cut 12 inches of ¼-inch-wide double-faced satin ribbon. Run the ribbon ends through the tops of miniature vintage or reproduction ornaments. Fold the ends back on themselves and glue them in place. Drape the ribbon over the tree branch.

◀ Button, Button: The humblest materials become charming when clustered together as a mini-collection. Clean out the button box or buy inexpensive crafting buttons by the tub. Sew or glue them to a star-shaped fabric background, packing them tightly so they overlap. Add a cord for hanging and a tassel at the bottom for an elegant touch.

◀ For Peat's Sake: Who would believe a garden peat pot could become an elegant ornament? Paint the pot with several coats of acrylic paint. Glue a reproduction vintage Christmas card to the pot. Brush the card and pot with a light coat of matte decoupage medium. While the medium is still wet, sprinkle the surface with glitter. Punch holes in the sides and hang the pot from wide ribbon. Fill the pot with evergreen sprigs, berry clusters, and tiny ornaments.

Crème de Menthe Brownies,
page 94

gathering together

so many days and ways to celebrate.

GATHERING *together*

Whatever your entertaining style—whether you keep it simple or pull out all the stops—and whatever holidays your family and friends celebrate, turn the page to find beautiful ways to dress up your space and table for company.

frosty family

Guests will giggle when greeted by a snowman family made from recycled jars filled with artificial snow.

snow family

1 Wash and dry the jars and lids, removing all residue. For each snowman, select two buttons for the eyes and five buttons for the mouth.

2 Place a dot of hot glue on a button. Quickly press the button to the inside of the jar for one of the eyes. For narrow jars, use long tweezers or needle-nose pliers to hold the buttons. Repeat for the other eye. Add the mouth buttons, giving each figure a different expression.

3 Roll a small piece of modeling material into a carrot shape for a nose. Use a table knife to make the indentations along the carrot. Make a different size nose for each snowman.

4 Fill each jar with artificial snow until it is full and well packed. After the noses dry, slide them into the jars, using the snow to hold them in place.

5 For the table mat, glue ball fringe onto a 16x27-inch piece of red felt. Using three plies of embroidery floss, randomly stitch simple snowflakes across the mat. Scatter green buttons over the mat and glue them in place, making sure to leave enough space for the jars. See the photograph *opposite* for details.

family hats

mom...

1 Cut a circle of felt several inches larger than the top of the jar. Glue the felt to the rim of the jar or lid, allowing it to puff slightly in the middle. Add a hatband of greenery and a small cluster of berries and other trims.

dad...

1 Cut a large circle of felt for the brim, a smaller circle for the top, and a rectangular strip for the tube. Glue the three pieces together. Glue the hat to the lid and add a hatband and clusters of berries, pinecones, and other trims.

kids...

1 For the hats, use only the cuff of the sock. Turn up 1 inch of the cuff for the hat band. Stretch the hat over the lid and glue it in place. Tie the open end with embroidery floss to form a stocking cap. Add pom-poms and other trims.

2 Cut the remaining sections of the socks into strips. Tie them around the jars for scarves. Glue on trims as desired.

What You'll Need...

- ☐ Various jars, preferably with lids
- ☐ Assorted buttons for eyes and mouths
- ☐ Hot-glue gun and glue sticks
- ☐ Long tweezers or needle-nose pliers (optional)
- ☐ Orange soft sponge-like modeling material
- ☐ Artificial snow
- ☐ ¾ yard of dark red brushed felt for the mat
- ☐ 2½ yards of ivory ball fringe
- ☐ Ecru embroidery floss
- ☐ Tapestry needle
- ☐ Dark green buttons
- ☐ Heavy felt for adult hats
- ☐ Small socks for children's hats and scarves
- ☐ Embroidery floss to match the socks
- ☐ Assorted trims for the hats and scarves

59

wrap it up

Give a centerpiece a sense of presence with fabric-wrapped boxes topped with elegant ribbons and trims.

What You'll Need...

☐ Sturdy empty boxes in a variety of sizes
☐ Coordinating fabrics for wrapping the boxes
☐ Hot-glue gun and glue sticks
☐ Coordinating ribbons
☐ Assorted greenery, Christmas ornaments, berries, pinecones, cinnamon sticks, raffia, jingle bells, and buttons

61

wraps with presence

Cover the boxes with fabric as if wrapping a package, trimming the excess bulk as needed and turning under the raw edges. Hot-glue all the seams and folds. Add coordinating ribbons, tacking them in place with glue. Using the packages shown on this page as inspiration, add various trims to each box. Glue the trims in place. The packages can be stored from year to year if they are trimmed in artificial, dried, or silk greens and berries.

NOTE: These embellishment ideas also can be used to create stunning gift wraps. Just substitute wrapping paper for the fabric.

◀ Stocking Stuffers: Miniature stockings keep flatware and napkins in place, making it easy for guests to go through a buffet line. Buy small versions or sew your own following general stocking sewing instructions, making the socks only about 12 inches long. Mix and match the fabrics to coordinate with your holiday dinnerware.

In a Twinkling:
tabletop

◀ Stars on Ice: Frozen cranberries chill a bottle of bubbly without turning into a puddle of water by evening's end. Star-shape ice cubes (made in special ice cube trays) add a festive touch to the berry bright arrangement.

62

▶ Picture Perfect: Fresh flowers suspended in a picture frame add elegance to a table without being obtrusive. Look for frames that stand upright on their own (without an easel back). At the last minute, trim the flower stems. Group several blooms together, loop satin ribbon around the frame, and wrap the ribbon ends to the stems.

▲ Naturally Elegant: A glorious fruit garland composed of honeydew, pineapple, grapes, pomelo, star fruit, quince, pears, and apples combines with evergreens, flowing ivy, and alstroemeria. The subtle blend of fragrances adds a warm sweetness to the room as the arrangement winds down the length of the table, highlighting fine china and crisp linens.

63

▲ Looking Back: Velvet ribbon and a sprig of fresh pepperberries give an elegant touch to the simplest of slipcovers. Tie the ribbon around the chair back just above the seat, creating a fitted look. Tuck the pepperberries into the knot of the bow.

Contemporary twists on traditional designs give an updated flair to Hanukkah decorations while staying true to the holiday's meaning.

the art of Hanukkah

Bring a fresh look to your home this Hanukkah with handmade items that have a decidedly artistic look. Stars of David, a menorah, and a dreidel embellish tabletop items. Invitations and companion place cards set the mood for a lively evening.

Trace the pattern on *page 157*

65

What You'll Need...

- ☐ Cobalt blue goblets
- ☐ Permanent glass etching cream, such as Armour Etch
- ☐ Clear self-adhesive vinyl sheets or shelf paper
- ☐ Crafts knife
- ☐ Disposable foam brush

What You'll Need...

- ☐ Paper-backed fusible transfer web
- ☐ Blue fabric for the star
- ☐ Purchased or self-made white napkin
- ☐ White embroidery floss and embroidery needle
- ☐ 18 inches of rattail cord

"gelt" napkin

1 Fuse the transfer web to the wrong side of the blue fabric. On the paper side of the web, draw a Star of David. Cut out the star. Peel off the paper backing, position the star on a napkin corner, and fuse it in place. See the photograph *opposite* for details. Blanket-stitch around the edge using white embroidery floss.

2 Fold the napkin in half diagonally. Accordion-pleat the flat edge. Tie the rattail cord around the napkin about two inches from the top. Tie knots in the ends of the rattail. Shape the napkin so it resembles a gelt bag.

3 To make a coordinating place mat, follow the napkin directions and fuse and stitch a white star to a place mat.

etched goblet

1 When using etching cream, follow the manufacturer's directions exactly. Clean and dry the glassware; set aside.

2 Trace the pattern on *page 157* onto the vinyl. Cut out the design, leaving 1 to 2 inches beyond the outer edge. Using a crafts knife, cut along all the design lines. Carefully press the adhesive to the glass, smoothing it to seal it tightly. Remove the gray portions of the design, exposing the glass. Seal the remaining vinyl again.

3 Apply the etching cream according to the manufacturer's directions. After the allotted time, wash off the cream. Allow a few minutes for the design to appear.

What You'll Need...

☐ 6¼×9-inch and 4×5-inch rectangles of glossy white card stock
☐ 6×4¼-inch piece of blue speckled paper
☐ Double-stick tape
☐ Scraps of metallic gold card stock
☐ Monofilament
☐ Paper adhesive or glue stick
☐ 6×4¼-inch piece of paper for the inside

Menorah invitation and card

1 Fold the large piece of white card stock in half crosswise. Center the blue speckled paper on the front of the card and join them with tape.

2 Enlarge, trace, and cut the menorah pattern *below* from the remaining white card stock. For the flames, cut nine elongated triangles from gold card stock.

3 Cut nine 1-inch lengths of monofilament. Glue one end of each piece of monofilament to the back of a flame and the other end to the back of a candle, leaving ⅛ to ⅜ inch of monofilament between the flame and candle. See the pattern for details.

4 Glue the menorah to the blue speckled paper, centering it and placing the flames in random positions.

5 Hand-write or computer-print the invitation or greeting on the inside paper. Center the paper on the inside of the card and join the pieces with tape.

ENLARGE PATTERN 200%

What You'll Need...

- ☐ Metallic silver and glossy white card stock
- ☐ Blue speckled paper
- ☐ Fine-tipped marking pens in white, blue, or silver
- ☐ Paper adhesive or glue stick
- ☐ Double-stick tape
- ☐ Crafts knife

place cards

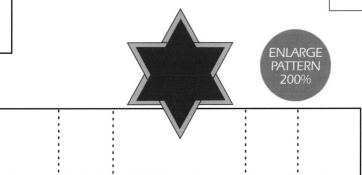

1 For the dreidel card, enlarge, trace, and cut a silver metallic dreidel using the pattern *below*. Mount the dreidel on blue paper. Trim the blue paper to leave ⅛ inch beyond the edge of the dreidel.

2 From glossy white, cut a 2¼×5½-inch rectangle. Fold the rectangle in half crosswise. Glue the dreidel to the front so it extends beyond the edge of the card. Hand-write the name.

1 For the wide Star of David card, enlarge, trace, and cut a wide Star of David from blue paper using the pattern *below*. Mount the star on white card stock. Trim the card stock to leave ⅛ inch beyond the blue star.

2 Cut a 1½×7¾-inch rectangle from white card stock. Fold under 2½ inches on each end, creating the card front. Fold 1⅜ inch on each end back forward, accordion style. This should make the card stand upright.

3 Glue the lower point of the star at the center front of the place card. Hand-write the name.

1 For the tall Star of David card, enlarge, trace, and cut out a tall Star of David from blue using the pattern *below*. Mount the star on silver paper. Trim the silver paper to leave ⅛ inch beyond the blue star.

2 Cut a 3¼×5½-inch rectangle from white card stock. Fold the rectangle in half crosswise. Glue the star to the card so it extends beyond the edges. Hand-write the name.

67

ENLARGE PATTERN 200%

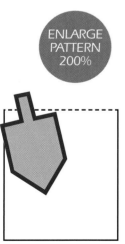

ENLARGE PATTERN 200%

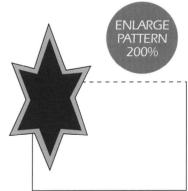

ENLARGE PATTERN 200%

Boursin Mashed
Potatoes
(see recipe, page

Maple-Brined Turkey,
Vegetable Medley
au Gratin,
Kumquat-Cranberry
Sauce
(see recipes, page 70)

68

the make-ahead

Make it delicious, make it memorable—and make it ahead!

This menu of holiday foods and storage tips give you even more reason to celebrate.

Our advice for the best holiday season ever? Two words: Make ahead. There's simply no better strategy for enjoying the merriment than to prepare little by little in the months, weeks, and days leading up to the holidays. While you're holiday shopping and working on homemade gifts and decorations, why not take care of the cooking too? When family and friends fill your home, you'll be able to fully partake in the joy and warmth of the holidays.

Experiment with these festive foods well in advance of your holiday meal— from three months to 24 hours ahead. In your recipe plans include one of the world's all-time best make-ahead desserts: cheesecake. Then fill your holiday table by applying the make-ahead strategy to your own favorite holiday recipes.

MAKE-AHEAD HOLIDAY TIMELINE

Up to 3 months ahead:
- Prepare Cornmeal Buns; freeze

Up to 1 month ahead:
- Prepare cheesecake; freeze
- Prepare cheese logs; freeze

Up to 2 days ahead:
- Prepare cranberry sauce; refrigerate

Up to 1 day ahead:
- Prepare soup; chill
- Thaw cheesecake and cheese log in refrigerator
- Begin brining turkey
- Prepare mashed potatoes; chill
- Prepare salad; chill
- Prepare vegetable medley; chill

3½ hours ahead:
- Roast turkey

1–2 hours ahead:
- Thaw Cornmeal Buns
- Reheat vegetable medley as directed

30 minutes ahead:
- Roll cheese log in nuts; let stand at room temperature as directed
- Remove turkey from oven; let stand at room temperature
- Reheat mashed potatoes in microwave as directed
- Bring cranberry sauce to room temperature

Just before serving:
- Carve turkey
- Reheat soup
- Toss salad

69

holiday

Maple-Brined Turkey

✳

Brining—soaking foods in salt-infused liquid—adds moisture and flavor to poultry. This recipe makes a very juicy bird. Start marinating up to 24 hours before roasting. Pictured on page 68.

- 1½ gallons water (24 cups)
- 1½ cups maple-flavored syrup
- 1 cup coarse salt
- ¾ cup packed brown sugar
- 1 10-pound turkey (not self-basting) Cooking oil

For brine, in a stockpot large enough to hold the turkey combine water, syrup, salt, and brown sugar; stir to dissolve salt and sugar.

Rinse turkey; remove any excess fat from cavity. Carefully add turkey to brine. Cover and marinate in the refrigerator at least 12 hours or up to 24 hours.

Remove turkey from brine; discard brine. Rinse turkey and pat dry with paper towels. Place turkey, breast up, on a rack in a roasting pan. Tuck the ends of the drumsticks under the band of skin across the tail. (If the band of skin is not present, tie the drumsticks securely to the tail.) Twist wing tips under the back. Brush with oil. Insert a meat thermometer into the center of one of the inside thigh muscles (the thermometer should not touch bone).

Cover turkey loosely with foil. Roast turkey in a 325°F oven for 2¾ to 3 hours or until thermometer registers 180°F. After 2¼ hours, remove foil and cut band of skin or string between the drumsticks so thighs will cook evenly. When done, drumsticks should move very easily in their sockets. Cover turkey; let stand at room temperature for 20 minutes before carving. Makes 12 servings.

Vegetable Medley au Gratin

✳

No need to peel and chop vegetables with this recipe—it starts with a convenient bag of frozen and precut broccoli, cauliflower, and carrots. You can get a head start on it the day before it's served. Pictured on page 68.

- 1 10¾-ounce can condensed cream of chicken and mushroom soup
- ½ cup dairy sour cream
- ½ teaspoon dried dill
- 2 16-ounce packages loose-pack frozen broccoli, cauliflower, and carrots, thawed
- ⅔ cup crushed stone-ground wheat crackers (about 15 crackers)
- ⅓ cup finely chopped walnuts or pecans
- ¼ cup finely shredded Parmesan cheese
- 2 tablespoons butter, melted

In a very large bowl combine condensed soup, sour cream, and dill; stir in thawed vegetables. Transfer to a 2-quart rectangular baking dish. Bake, covered, in a 325°F oven for 45 minutes.

In a small bowl combine crackers, walnuts, Parmesan cheese, and melted butter. Uncover baking dish; sprinkle cracker mixture over vegetable mixture. Increase oven temperature to 375°F. Bake, uncovered, about 15 minutes more or until heated through and topping is browned. Makes 10 servings.

To Make Ahead: Prepare, cover, and chill vegetable and crumb mixtures separately overnight before baking.

Kumquat-Cranberry Sauce

✳

Resembling miniature round oranges, fresh kumquats begin appearing in markets during November—just in time to add their bright, sweet-tart spark to a traditional holiday relish. Pictured on page 68.

- 12 ounces fresh kumquats, halved crosswise and seeded (2 cups)
- 1 cup packed brown sugar
- 1 cup cranberry juice
- 2 inches stick cinnamon
- 8 ounces fresh cranberries (2 cups)

In a large saucepan combine kumquats, brown sugar, cranberry juice, and stick cinnamon. Bring mixture to boiling; reduce heat. Simmer, uncovered, about 3 minutes or until kumquats are slightly softened.

Stir in cranberries. Bring to boiling; reduce heat. Simmer, uncovered, for 5 to 6 minutes more or until syrup begins to thicken. Remove stick cinnamon; serve sauce warm or at room temperature. Makes 3¼ cups.

To Make Ahead: Prepare Kumquat-Cranberry Sauce as directed. Cover and chill in the refrigerator for up to 2 days. To serve, let sauce stand at room temperature for 30 minutes before serving. Or transfer sauce to a small saucepan. Heat, uncovered, over medium-low heat until heated through, stirring occasionally.

70

Smoky Cheese Logs

Smoky Cheese Logs

✳

These cheese logs freeze beautifully for multiple menus. Serve one now and freeze the other. Or freeze them both— thaw one for your holiday meal and reserve one for a New Year's celebration.

  2 8-ounce packages cream
     cheese
  2 cups finely shredded smoked
     cheddar, Swiss, or Gouda
     cheese
 ½ cup butter or margarine
  2 tablespoons milk
  2 teaspoons steak sauce
  1 cup sliced almonds or other
     nuts, toasted
    Assorted crackers

In a large mixing bowl let cream cheese, shredded cheese, and butter stand at room temperature for 30 minutes. Add milk and steak sauce; beat with an electric mixer on medium speed until fluffy. Divide in half. Cover and chill for 4 to 24 hours.

Shape each half into a 6-inch-long log; roll logs in nuts. Let stand for 15 minutes. Serve with crackers. Makes 3½ cups.

To Make Ahead: Prepare as above, except do not roll in nuts. Wrap cheese logs in moistureproof and vaporproof plastic wrap. Freeze for up to 1 month. To serve, thaw in refrigerator overnight. Roll in nuts. Let stand for 30 minutes at room temperature before serving.

Treats in Store

Before the flurry and fun of the gift-giving season, wrap and freeze some goodies to share with friends later. Here are some general guidelines for how long fresh-baked holiday treats can be frozen:

- Cookies (unfrosted): up to 3 months
- Cheesecakes (whole): up to 1 month
- Layer cakes (unfrosted): up to 3 months
- Muffins and quick breads: up to 3 months
- Yeast breads: up to 3 months
- Fruitcakes: up to 12 months
- Fruit pies (unbaked): up to 4 months
- Fruit pies (baked): up to 4 months

Beet and Apple Salad

More Ways to Plan Ahead

■ Set the table the day before; choose your serving platters and bowls, and have them ready and waiting, perhaps in a pantry or nearby room out of the way until you need them. When it's time to bring foods to the table, you'll have just the dish you want.

■ Think through the entire flow of the meal and prepare whatever you can—from setting up the corkscrew, glasses, and hors d'oeuvres plates to lining a breadbasket and grinding beans for after-dinner coffee.

■ Remember that even when a recipe can't be made entirely in advance, perhaps some aspects can. Read through each recipe to determine which steps you can take ahead—such as toasting nuts, roasting red peppers, or preparing piecrust or sauce.

■ Tend to essentials first: Do what is absolutely necessary to pull off a joyful holiday meal. When you have extra time, add the beautiful garnishes you see in photographs—providing you're not cutting into time that you could be spending with family and friends.

Beet and Apple Salad

✳

Prepare the beets, mix the salad dressing, and tear up the romaine up to 24 hours in advance. The apples will brown if cut in advance, so chop and toss those just before serving.

  3 medium beets (about 1 pound total) or one 16-ounce can julienne beets, rinsed and drained
  ⅓ cup salad oil
  ⅓ cup white wine vinegar
  2 teaspoons finely shredded orange peel
  ¼ cup orange juice
  2 green onions, sliced (¼ cup)
  2 tablespoons snipped fresh mint or 2 teaspoons dried mint, crushed
  2 teaspoons honey
  6 cups torn romaine lettuce
  2 medium tart green apples, coarsely chopped

If using whole beets, in a large saucepan combine beets and enough water to cover. Bring to boiling; reduce heat. Simmer, covered, for 40 to 50 minutes or until tender; drain. Cool slightly; slip off skins and cut into thin bite-size strips.

Meanwhile, for dressing, in a screw-top jar, combine salad oil, vinegar, orange peel, orange juice, green onions, mint, and honey. Cover and shake well.

In a medium bowl, combine beet strips and ¼ cup of the dressing. Cover and refrigerate the beet mixture and the remaining dressing for at least 2 hours or up to 24 hours.

To serve, in a large bowl combine torn romaine and chopped apples. Toss lettuce and apple mixture with the remaining dressing. Using a slotted spoon, layer beet mixture over apple mixture in bowl. Makes 8 servings.

Four-Onion Soup

✳

Leeks, onions, garlic, and a sprinkling of chives—those are the four varieties of onion here. You'll love the way the first three mellow and deepen in flavor in this rich, elegant first-course soup.

  ¼ cup butter
  3 cups thinly sliced leeks (white
       part only) (9 to 10 leeks)
4½ cups halved and thinly sliced
       onions (3 to 4 large onions)
  2 tablespoons minced garlic
       (12 cloves)
  1 tablespoon sugar
  6 cups chicken broth
  1 teaspoon dried thyme, crushed
  ¼ teaspoon black pepper
  2 tablespoons all-purpose flour
  2 slightly beaten egg yolks
  ¼ cup Marsala wine or sweet
       sherry (optional)
  1 cup half-and-half or light cream
       Baguette-style French bread
       slices, toasted (optional)
       Fresh chives (optional)
       Fresh thyme (optional)

In a 4-quart Dutch oven melt butter over medium-low heat. Stir in leeks, onions, garlic, and sugar. Cook, covered, over medium-low heat for about 10 minutes or until tender, stirring occasionally. Remove ¾ cup of the onion-leek mixture; set aside. Add 5½ cups of the broth, the dried thyme, and pepper to remaining mixture in Dutch oven. Bring to boiling; reduce heat. Simmer, covered, over low heat for 20 minutes.

Remove from heat; cool slightly. Transfer one-third of the broth mixture to a blender container or food processor bowl. Cover and blend or process until the mixture is smooth. Repeat with remaining mixture. Return all of the pureed mixture to the Dutch oven. Heat just to boiling.

In a small bowl stir together the remaining ½ cup broth and flour until smooth. Stir in egg yolks. Gradually add 1 cup of the hot soup to egg mixture; stir this mixture into the soup in the Dutch oven. Cook and stir over medium-high heat until thickened and bubbly. Add Marsala, if desired, and reserved onion-leek mixture. Cook and stir for 1 minute more; reduce heat. Stir in half-and-half.* Cook and stir until heated through; do not boil.

To serve, ladle into a large soup tureen or serving-size bowls. Top each serving with a toasted baguette slice, if desired. Sprinkle soup with chives and thyme, if desired. Makes 8 side-dish servings.

*To Make Ahead: At this point, cover and refrigerate the soup for up to 24 hours. At serving time, heat through; do not boil.

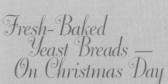

Fresh-Baked Yeast Breads — On Christmas Day

The dilemma: You love serving home-made breads and dinner rolls, but who has time to mix, knead, punch, and rise dough on Christmas day?

The solution: Prepare the dough in advance. Just follow the recipe through mixing and kneading stages. Form the dough into a ball; wrap it in moisture-proof and vaporproof wrap or place it in a self-sealing freezer bag. Chill dough up to 24 hours; bring dough to room temperature before shaping. Or freeze the dough up to 3 months. Thaw frozen dough at room temperature up to 2 hours or in the refrigerator overnight. Shape and bake according to the recipe.

73

Four-Onion Soup

Boursin Mashed Potatoes

✳

These perfect potatoes are so creamy and rich, they can be served on their own— no last-minute gravy-making flurry needed! Prepare them ahead; reheat in a microwave oven just before serving. Pictured on page 68.

3½ pounds potatoes, peeled and cut into 2-inch chunks (about 10 medium potatoes)
2 5.2-ounce packages boursin cheese with garlic and herbs
½ cup whole milk, half-and-half, or light cream
Salt and black pepper

In a large saucepan or Dutch oven cover potatoes with water. Cook, covered, for 20 to 25 minutes or until tender. Drain; return potatoes to saucepan or Dutch oven. Mash with potato masher or beat with mixer on low speed until smooth. Add cheese; beat until combined. Beat in milk until combined. Season with salt and pepper. Spoon potato mixture into a 2-quart baking dish.

Cover and bake in a 350°F oven for 25 minutes or until heated through. Makes 8 to 10 servings.

To Make Ahead: Prepare Boursin Mashed Potatoes as directed through seasoning. Spoon potatoes into a microwave-safe 2-quart casserole. Cover; refrigerate up to 24 hours. To serve, uncover potatoes. Cover with vented plastic wrap. Microwave on 100-percent power (high) for 15 to 18 minutes or until heated through, stirring once. (Or bake, covered, in a 350°F oven about 1½ hours or until heated through.)

Cornmeal Buns

✳

Here's a light cornmeal-infused take on ever-popular dinner rolls. Choose from two make-ahead strategies: Prepare the dough ahead and bake the buns fresh the day of your holiday meal (see tip, page 73). Or bake them ahead, freeze up to 3 months, thaw at room temperature, and gently warm them in the oven.

6 to 6½ cups all-purpose flour
1 package active dry yeast
2¼ cups milk
½ cup sugar
½ cup butter
1 teaspoon salt
2 eggs
1½ cups cornmeal

In a large mixing bowl combine 3 cups of the flour and the yeast. In a saucepan heat milk, sugar, butter, and salt just until warm (115°F to 120°F), stirring constantly to melt butter. Add milk mixture to flour mixture in mixing bowl; add eggs. Beat with an electric mixer on low speed for 30 seconds, scraping bowl constantly. Beat on high speed for 3 minutes. Turn to low speed and beat in cornmeal. Stir in as much remaining flour as you can with a wooden spoon.

Turn dough onto a lightly floured surface. Knead in enough remaining flour to make a moderately stiff dough that is smooth and elastic (6 to 8 minutes total). Shape dough into a ball. Place in a greased bowl; turn once. Cover; let rise in a warm place until doubled in size (1 to 1¼ hours). Grease thirty-six 2½-inch muffin cups.

Punch down dough. Turn dough onto a lightly floured surface. Shape into 72 balls. Place 2 balls in each prepared muffin cup. Cover; let rise until nearly double (50 to 60 minutes).

Bake in a 375°F oven for 12 to 15 minutes or until rolls are golden brown. Immediately remove from pans to wire racks. Serve warm or cooled. Makes 36 buns.

Tip: If you have fewer than 36 muffin cups, place dough balls on a waxed paper-lined baking sheet; cover with plastic wrap and chill while the first pan rises and bakes. After removing the baked rolls from pans, wash pan, grease, and refill each cup with remaining chilled dough. Cover, let rise, and bake as directed above.

Make-Ahead Cheesecake

Cheesecake is the ultimate make-ahead dessert. Not only can it be refrigerated up to 3 days ahead of time, but it also freezes well. Here are some storage tips.

■ To refrigerate cheesecake: Cover thoroughly with plastic wrap. It will stay fresh in the refrigerator up to 3 days.

■ To freeze cheesecake: Seal a whole cheesecake or slices in a freezer bag in an airtight container or wrapped in heavy foil. Freeze up to 1 month. To thaw, loosen the covering slightly; thaw in the refrigerator for 24 hours.

■ Freeze leftover cheesecake slices up to 2 weeks, thawing a slice at a time for an indulgent treat. Seal slices in a freezer bag, airtight container, or wrapped in heavy foil. Thaw at room temperature about 30 minutes.

Mint-Chocolate Chip Cheesecake

Mint-Chocolate Chip Cheesecake

✳

This beautiful green-tinted cheesecake looks as festive as it is refreshing. The flavors, a cool combination of chocolate and mint, are the perfect palate pleasers!

2 cups finely crushed chocolate wafers (about 36 to 38 wafers)
½ cup butter, melted
2 8-ounce packages cream cheese, softened
1 cup sugar
¼ cup green crème de menthe liqueur
3 eggs
3 8-ounce cartons dairy sour cream
1 cup miniature semisweet chocolate pieces (6 ounces)
1 ounce semisweet chocolate
1 teaspoon shortening

In a mixing bowl combine crushed wafers and butter; toss gently. Press wafer mixture on bottom and 2 inches up sides of a 9-inch springform pan. Set aside.

For filling, in a large mixing bowl beat cream cheese and sugar with an electric mixer until combined. Beat in crème de menthe. Add eggs all at once, beating on low speed just until combined. Stir in sour cream until combined; stir in the 1 cup semisweet chocolate pieces.

Pour filling into crust-lined pan. Set the pan on a shallow baking pan on the oven rack. Bake in a 375°F oven for 50 to 55 minutes or until the center appears nearly set when gently shaken (filling will puff and settle as it cools).

Remove springform pan from baking pan. Cool cheesecake in springform pan on a wire rack for 15 minutes. Use a small metal spatula to loosen crust from sides of pan. Cool 30 minutes more. Gently remove springform sides of pan. Cool for 1 hour; cover and chill at least 4 hours.

For topping, in a small saucepan melt the 1 ounce semisweet chocolate and the shortening over low heat. Drizzle chocolate over chilled cheesecake. Chill until set. Makes 14 to 16 servings.

MAKE-AHEAD TIPS: Crush wafers up to 1 day before using. Place crushed wafers in a covered container and store at room temperature. See the tips, *opposite,* for how to refrigerate and freeze cheesecakes.

Festive Chicken Liver and Pear Spread
(see recipe, page 78)

*Lamb Meatballs with Minted
Cucumber-Yogurt Sauce*
(see recipe, page 80)

Fall and winter mark the time of meaningful celebrations by many people of diverse cultures. This season, enrich your holiday experience by inviting friends to gather around a table filled with foods that represent a variety of heritages.

a multicultural potluck

Enhance your holiday celebration with a multicultural potluck. Start by encouraging people you know to bring dishes indicative of their religious or cultural traditions. Guests who celebrate Christmas can bring foods specific to their ancestry. From Russia to Mexico, the holiday represents a rich assortment of foods—and your buffet can reflect those flavorful nuances.

As host, you may need to add a few dishes to balance out the meal. The selections on the following pages are inspired by Hanukkah, Ramadan, and Kwanzaa traditions; peruse the other recipes in this book for additional Christmas ideas.

Another approach is to gather a "cooking team." Prepare the recipes on these pages together, filling out the menu with your own cherished food traditions. Then treat all your guests to an exquisite sampling of holiday foods.

To better understand the ethnic foods you prepare, learn more about these cultural and religious celebrations:

Christmas: For Christians, this holiday recognizes the birth of Jesus Christ. Diverse celebrations around the world include decorations, gifts, and special foods that people serve only at that time. The season begins with Advent and ends with Epiphany (January 6), which celebrates the Wise Men's journey to the Christ child.

Hanukkah: In Hebrew this word means "dedication." The holiday observes the event 2,000 years ago when Jews rededicated the Temple of Jerusalem following its desecration. To rekindle the menorah, a symbol of a covenant between God and the Jewish people, there was only enough oil to burn for one night, but miraculously it lasted for eight nights. Jews recall the miracle and the story of survival by lighting candles eight successive nights.

Kwanzaa: Beginning the day after Christmas and lasting through January 1, Kwanzaa honors African-American history, culture, and ties between family and friends. During the celebration, the focus is on nurturing a sense of identity, community, and self-esteem. Foods inspired by rich culinary traditions of Africa, America, the Caribbean, and South America play a meaningful role. The holiday culminates in a feast, karamu, on December 31.

Ramadan: This holiday is a time of worship, contemplation, and renewing of family and community bonds. Muslims observe this holy period during the ninth month of the Muslim calendar. By fasting from before sunrise until after sundown, they effect a sympathetic reminder of the sufferings of others, then break the fast with small meals shared among family and friends. Providing food and drink after sundown to those who are fasting is considered honorable and empathetic.

Festive Chicken Liver and Pear Spread

✳

Chopped liver is a popular Jewish-American dish. This appetizer dresses up the ordinary standby with pears, nuts, dried fruits, and just the right seasonings. Pictured on page 76.

    1 pound chicken livers
    1 tablespoon olive oil, margarine,
         or butter
  ¾ cup chopped, peeled pear
         (1 medium)
  ½ cup chopped onion
    6 cloves garlic, minced
         (1 tablespoon)
    1 tablespoon white wine vinegar
  ½ teaspoon salt
  ½ teaspoon ground black pepper
  ½ teaspoon ground allspice
  ⅓ cup toasted hazelnuts*,
         chopped
  ⅔ cup dried cranberries, golden
         raisins, and/or snipped
         dried apricots
       Snipped fresh parsley

Rinse chicken livers under cold running water; pat dry with paper towels. Remove fat and connective tissue from livers. In a large skillet heat olive oil over medium heat. Add chicken livers, pear, onion, and garlic to skillet. Cook and stir for 10 to 12 minutes or until livers are no longer pink. Cool slightly (about 10 minutes).

Transfer liver mixture to a food processor. Add vinegar, salt, pepper, and allspice. Cover and process until smooth. Line a 3-cup soufflé dish, straight-sided mold, or 6-inch springform pan with plastic wrap. Spoon in liver mixture. Cover and chill for 4 to 24 hours.

To serve, uncover liver mixture and invert onto a small platter. Carefully remove plastic wrap. Gently press nuts onto sides of liver mixture. Arrange the dried fruit and parsley on the top of the mixture, making a decorative pattern. Gently press down fruit and parsley into the liver mixture. Makes 2 cups (32 one-tablespoon servings).

***Note:** To toast hazelnuts, spread the nuts in a single layer in a shallow baking pan. Bake, uncovered, in a 350°F oven for 8 to 10 minutes, stirring once or twice, until portions of nuts visible through skin appear lightly browned. Immediately spread nuts on a clean kitchen towel. Fold towel over nuts; rub gently with towel to remove skins.

Fattoush

✳

Fattoush is a favorite Middle Eastern bread, tomato, and cucumber salad. During Ramadan, a big salad bowl is often a colorful part of the iftar—the evening meal at which the day's fast is broken.

    2 large pita bread rounds, split
         in half
    1 medium cucumber, halved
         lengthwise and thinly sliced
         (1¾ cups)
  1½ cups grape tomatoes, halved
         (8 ounces)
    1 medium yellow and/or green
         sweet pepper, cut into bite-
         size strips (1 cup)
  ¼ cup finely chopped red or
         yellow onion
  ¼ cup thinly sliced green
         onions (2)
  ⅓ cup olive oil
    3 tablespoons lemon juice
    1 tablespoon snipped
         fresh parsley
    1 tablespoon snipped fresh mint
  ½ teaspoon salt
  ¼ teaspoon freshly ground
         black pepper
    4 cups torn romaine leaves

Place pita bread rounds on a large baking sheet so they do not overlap. Bake rounds in a 350°F oven for about 10 minutes or until dry and crisp. Cool on a wire rack. Break into bite-size pieces. Set aside.

In a large bowl combine cucumber, tomatoes, sweet pepper, red onion, and green onions. Toss gently to combine.

In a screw-top jar combine olive oil, lemon juice, parsley, mint, salt, and black pepper. Cover; shake well. Pour dressing over vegetable mixture, tossing to mix. Cover and chill for 2 to 4 hours.

Just before serving, add the romaine leaves and toasted pita bread to the vegetables in the bowl; toss gently to mix. If desired, transfer salad to a large platter or to serving-size bowls to serve. Makes 8 to 10 servings.

78

Fattoush

Pulled Beef and Vegetable Sandwiches

Carefully remove ribs from Dutch oven and set aside to cool slightly. Add tomatoes and raisins to cooking liquid in Dutch oven. Bring to boiling; reduce heat. Boil gently, uncovered, over medium to medium-high heat about 45 minutes or until mixture begins to thicken.

Meanwhile, using two forks, pull beef to shred. Add shredded beef to vegetable mixture. Heat through. Serve on rolls with horseradish, if desired. Makes 12 to 16 sandwiches.

*NOTE: To prepare fennel, remove any wilted outer layers and cut a thin slice from the fennel base. Wash fennel and cut into lengthwise quarters; remove core and discard. Chop remaining fennel.

80

Pulled Beef and Vegetable Sandwiches

✳

These luscious and varied sandwiches are a potluck hit any time of year! The tender, flavorful meat is similar to that of beef brisket—a signature Hanukkah dish. Tip: If you like, transfer the shredded meat mixture to a slow cooker to keep it warm for transporting.

- 3 pounds boneless beef ribs
- ½ teaspoon salt
- ½ teaspoon freshly ground black pepper
- 2 tablespoons olive oil
- 1½ cups sliced celery
- 1½ cups chopped onions
- 1 cup chopped carrots
- 1 cup chopped fresh fennel*
- 4 cloves garlic, minced
- 3 cups beef broth
- 1½ cups dry red wine
- 1 tablespoon packed brown sugar
- 2 teaspoons dried thyme, crushed
- 1 teaspoon dried rosemary, crushed
- 1 14½-ounce can petite diced tomatoes, undrained
- 1 cup golden raisins
- 12 to 16 French-style rolls
  Prepared horseradish (optional)

Trim fat, if present, from meat. In a small bowl stir together salt and pepper. Rub mixture evenly over all sides of ribs. In a 4-quart Dutch oven brown half the ribs at a time in hot oil. Set meat aside, reserving drippings in pan.

Cook celery, onions, carrots, fennel, and garlic in drippings in Dutch oven until tender, stirring occasionally.

Return all ribs to Dutch oven. Carefully add beef broth, wine, brown sugar, thyme, and rosemary. Bring to boiling; reduce heat. Simmer, covered, for 2 to 2½ hours or until beef is very tender. (Or bake, covered, in a 325°F oven for about 2½ hours or until beef is tender.)

Lamb Meatballs with Minted Cucumber-Yogurt Sauce

✳

In honor of Ramadan, these fun little nibbles are a welcome bite after a day of fasting. Or serve them anytime for an intriguing Mediterranean-inspired appetizer. Pictured on page 76.

- ¼ cup finely chopped onion
- 2 cloves garlic, minced
- 2 teaspoons olive oil
- 1 egg, slightly beaten
- ¼ cup fine dry bread crumbs
- ⅓ cup chopped toasted pine nuts
- 2 teaspoons finely snipped fresh mint
- ½ teaspoon salt
- ¼ teaspoon ground allspice
- ⅛ teaspoon ground cinnamon
- ⅛ teaspoon ground black pepper
- 1 pound ground lamb or ground beef
  Minted Cucumber-Yogurt Sauce (see opposite)

In a small skillet cook and stir onion and garlic in hot oil about 3 minutes or until tender but not brown. Remove onion mixture from heat.

In a large bowl combine egg, bread crumbs, pine nuts, onion mixture, mint, salt, allspice, cinnamon, and pepper; stir to mix. Add ground meat to mixture in the bowl; mix well.

Shape meat mixture into thirty-six ¾-inch-diameter meatballs (to keep meatballs from sticking to your hands, wet hands slightly). Arrange meatballs in a 15×10×1-inch baking pan. Bake, uncovered, in a 350°F oven for 20 minutes. Drain off fat. Using a metal spatula, transfer meatballs to a serving dish. Serve with Minted Cucumber-Yogurt Sauce. Makes 36 meatballs.

MINTED CUCUMBER-YOGURT SAUCE: In a small bowl stir together one 8-ounce carton plain yogurt; ¼ cup coarsely shredded unpeeled cucumber, drained*; 1 clove garlic, minced; 1 tablespoon finely snipped fresh mint; ⅛ teaspoon salt; and a dash of ground black pepper. Cover and chill for up to 24 hours. Stir before serving.

***NOTE:** To prevent the sauce from becoming too watery, be sure to drain the cucumber.

Chicken and Fruit Couscous

✳

When family and friends gather to break the fast during Ramadan, meals often center on lamb, beef, or chicken. Using turmeric and other earthy spices as well as couscous, dried fruits, and nuts, this dish is influenced by North African cooking.

  1 teaspoon salt
  1 teaspoon ground cumin
  1 teaspoon ground ginger
  ½ teaspoon turmeric
  ½ teaspoon ground cinnamon
  6 boneless, skinless chicken breast halves, cut into 1-inch pieces
  1 tablespoon olive oil

  2 tablespoons butter
  3 medium onions, cut into thin wedges (1½ cups)
  4 cloves garlic, minced
  ¼ teaspoon crushed red pepper
  1 6-ounce package dried apricots, cut into strips
  ¾ cup golden raisins
  3 14-ounce cans chicken broth
  1 10-ounce package quick-cooking couscous
  ¼ teaspoon ground black pepper
  ⅔ cup slivered or sliced almonds, toasted
     Fresh flat-leaf parsley

For spice mixture, in a small bowl stir together salt, cumin, ginger, turmeric, and cinnamon. Sprinkle 1 tablespoon of the spice mixture over the chicken. Cover and chill for 1 to 2 hours to allow spices to penetrate meat. Set aside the remaining spice mixture.

In a 4-quart Dutch oven heat oil over medium-high heat. Add half of the chicken to Dutch oven. Cook and stir

for 4 to 5 minutes or until chicken is no longer pink. Remove chicken. (If necessary, add additional olive oil.) Cook remaining chicken as above. Remove chicken; set aside.

Add butter to Dutch oven and melt over medium-high heat. Add onions, garlic, and crushed red pepper. Cook about 8 minutes or until onions begin to turn golden, stirring occasionally. Add remaining spice mixture to onion mixture, stirring to combine. Return chicken to Dutch oven along with apricots and raisins.

Add broth to Dutch oven. Bring to boiling. Stir in couscous and black pepper. Cover and remove from heat. Let stand for 5 minutes. Just before serving, sprinkle chicken and couscous mixture with almonds and garnish with parsley. Makes 8 to 10 servings.

81

Chicken and Fruit Couscous

Holiday Noodle Kugel

Kugel is a Jewish dish, usually made with noodles and often served on the Sabbath. This kugel is a luscious accompaniment to roasted meats any time of year.

- 12 ounces wide egg noodles
- ¼ cup butter
- 3 cups chopped peeled apples
- 1 cup chopped onions
- ¾ cup chopped pitted whole dates
- ¾ cup dried tart red cherries
- 3 eggs, beaten
- 1 12-ounce carton cream-style cottage cheese
- 1 8-ounce carton dairy sour cream
- ⅓ cup sugar
- 1 tablespoon finely shredded orange peel
- 1 teaspoon vanilla
- ½ teaspoon salt
- ½ cup chopped walnuts
- 2 tablespoons sugar
- ¼ teaspoon ground cinnamon
- 2 tablespoon butter, melted

Cook noodles according to package directions; drain well and return to saucepan.

Meanwhile, in a large skillet melt the ¼ cup butter over medium-high heat. Add apples and onions. Cook for 3 minutes, stirring occasionally. Remove from heat. Stir in dates and cherries. Set aside.

In a large bowl stir together eggs, cottage cheese, sour cream, the ⅓ cup sugar, orange peel, vanilla, and salt. Add noodles and fruit mixture to egg mixture in bowl, gently stirring to coat. Transfer noodle mixture to a lightly greased 3-quart rectangular baking dish.

In a small bowl stir together walnuts, the 2 tablespoons sugar, and cinnamon. Sprinkle over noodle mixture. Drizzle the 2 tablespoons melted butter over the noodle mixture. Bake in a 350°F oven, uncovered, about 45 minutes or until top is golden. Makes 12 servings.

Pineapple Cake

Kwanzaa means "first fruits of harvest," and coconut is one of the token fruits of the celebration. With its shower of coconut, this flavorful cake fits right into the festivities.

- 1 20-ounce can crushed pineapple
- 2½ cups all-purpose flour
- 1½ teaspoons baking powder
- ½ teaspoon baking soda
- ¼ teaspoon salt
- ½ cup butter, softened
- 1 cup granulated sugar
- 2 eggs
- ¾ cup packed brown sugar
- ¾ cup chopped pecans
- ¾ cup coconut

Drain pineapple, reserving juice. In a medium bowl combine flour, baking powder, baking soda, and salt; set aside.

In a large mixing bowl beat the butter with an electric mixer on medium to high speed for 30 seconds. Add granulated sugar; beat until fluffy. Add eggs; beat until smooth. Alternately add flour mixture and reserved pineapple juice to egg mixture, beating at low speed after each addition just until combined. Fold in pineapple. Spread batter in a greased 13×9×2-inch baking pan or dish.

In a small bowl combine brown sugar, pecans, and coconut. Sprinkle over batter. Bake in a 350°F oven about 35 minutes or until a toothpick inserted in center comes out clean. Serve warm. Makes 12 to 16 servings.

82

Holiday Noodle Kugel

Sweet Potato Gingerbread Cake Roll

✳

Kwanzaa menus bring together foods from Africa, the Caribbean, and the American South. Sweet potatoes—native to the Caribbean and a close cousin to the yams grown in Africa—are a natural for the celebration. Here, the tuber is rolled into a luscious, springy cake.

    Nonstick cooking spray
 1 cup all-purpose flour
 1 teaspoon ground cinnamon
 ¾ teaspoon baking soda
 ¾ teaspoon baking powder
 ½ teaspoon ground ginger
 ¼ teaspoon ground cloves
 ⅛ teaspoon salt
 3 egg yolks
 ½ cup mild-flavored molasses
 1 tablespoon butter, melted
 1 teaspoon vanilla
 3 egg whites
 ¼ cup granulated sugar
 ¾ cup finely shredded sweet
       potato
    Sifted powdered sugar
 1½ cups whipping cream
 ⅓ cup sifted powdered sugar
 1 teaspoon ground cinnamon
 1 teaspoon vanilla
 ⅛ teaspoon ground cloves
 ¼ cup chopped pecans, toasted
    Orange peel curls

Coat a 15×10×1-inch baking pan with cooking spray. Line pan with waxed paper. Coat waxed paper with cooking spray. Lightly flour; set aside.

In a medium bowl combine flour, 1 teaspoon cinnamon, baking soda, baking powder, ½ teaspoon ginger, ¼ teaspoon cloves, and salt; set aside.

In a medium mixing bowl, beat egg yolks with an electric mixer on high speed for 5 minutes or until thick and lemon-color. Beat in molasses, melted butter, and 1 teaspoon of the vanilla just until combined.

Sweet Potato Gingerbread Cake Roll

83

Thoroughly wash and dry beaters. In another mixing bowl, beat egg whites on medium speed until soft peaks form (tips curl). Gradually add granulated sugar, beating until stiff peaks form (tips stand straight). Fold egg yolk mixture into egg whites. Sprinkle flour mixture over egg mixture; fold in gently just until combined. Fold in sweet potato. Spread batter evenly in prepared pan.

Bake in a 350°F oven for about 10 minutes or until cake springs back when lightly touched. Immediately loosen edges of cake from pan and turn out onto a clean cotton towel sprinkled with powdered sugar. Carefully remove waxed paper from cake. Starting from one short side of the cake, roll up towel and cake into a spiral. Cool on wire rack. Unroll cake.

In a chilled medium mixing bowl combine the whipping cream, the ⅓ cup powdered sugar, 1 teaspoon cinnamon, 1 teaspoon vanilla, and ⅛ teaspoon ground cloves. Beat with chilled beaters of an electric mixer on medium speed until soft peaks form.

Spread cake with half of the whipped cream, spreading to within 1 inch of edges. Roll up cake without towel. Evenly spread remaining whipped cream over rolled cake. Garnish with chopped pecans and orange peel curls. Chill for up to 2 hours. Makes 10 servings.

What You'll Need...

- [ ] Foam core board larger than the finished size of the mat
- [ ] Fusible interfacing the desired finished size of the mat
- [ ] 7/8- and 3/8-inch-wide grosgrain ribbon in sage green and 3/8-inch-wide ribbon in colonial blue
- [ ] Wood-burning tool
- [ ] Pins

multicultural crafts

Woven mats, a traditional symbol of Kwanzaa, take on a new-world look when blue and green ribbons take the place of Kwanzaa's multicolored grasses. Weave several to fit different serving tables or to overlap on one large buffet setting.

traditional mat

1 Measure the diameter of your table top or the desired size of the woven portion of the mat. Draw this dimension onto the foam core board. Draw a second set of lines 4 inches outside the initial drawing to allow ribbon "fringe" to drape over the table edge. Cut a piece of interfacing to fit the inside dimensions; set it aside.

2 Cut the ribbons to fit the outside measurements. NOTE: Cut the ribbon using a wood-burning tool, which slices through the ribbon and seals the edges simultaneously. Pin the vertical row of ribbons to the foam core board following the photograph *left*. The sides of the ribbons should go only to the inner lines, but the ends should extend to the outer lines.

3 Weave the horizontal ribbons through the vertical ribbons. Pin the ribbons together, as necessary, to keep them from sliding apart.

4 Remove the board. Fuse the interfacing to the woven portion of the mat to hold the ribbons in place.

What You'll Need...

- ☐ Blue and green tissue or rice paper
- ☐ 2¼-inch-diameter wooden doll head
- ☐ Decoupage medium
- ☐ Disposable foam brushes
- ☐ Awl and hammer
- ☐ Drill and ¹⁄₁₆-inch bit
- ☐ Green-color copper anodized wire
- ☐ Industrial-strength glue

card holder

1 Tear the papers into small irregular squares. Brush a doll head with decoupage medium and smooth the blue paper over the head. The paper will wrinkle and pucker as you arrange it. Add a light coat of decoupage medium over the paper.

2 Paint the ball with one more coat of decoupage medium. While the decoupage medium is still wet, place a few pieces of green paper over the blue paper. Add several more coats of decoupage medium, allowing each coat to dry according to the decoupage manufacturer's directions.

3 Using an awl and hammer, make a small pilot hole in the top of the doll head. Drill into the head at this point.

4 Shape the wire into two or three loops for holding the card, leaving long tails. Twist the tails together and cut the ends even. Dip the ends into the glue and insert them into the hole.

Brownie Waffles à la Mode

Plug in your waffle iron and heat up the holidays with these creative recipes—from bed-and-breakfast-style morning treats that make houseguests feel special to irresistible spicy cookies, chocolatey desserts, and warm suppers after a busy shopping day.

'tis the season for waffles!

Brownie Waffles à la Mode

✳

This recipe is a variation of the delicious brownie sundae. Pretty peppermint-stick ice cream and waffle-stamped brownies dress up the dish for the holidays. At another time of year, omit the peppermint and use your favorite flavor of premium ice cream—coffee is irresistible!

- 2 pints vanilla ice cream, softened
- ½ cup crushed striped round peppermint candies
- ¼ cup butter
- 2 ounces unsweetened baking chocolate, chopped
- ½ cup all-purpose flour
- ¼ cup unsweetened cocoa powder
- ¼ teaspoon baking powder
- ¼ teaspoon baking soda
- ¼ teaspoon salt
- 2 eggs
- ⅔ cup sugar
- ¼ cup half-and-half or light cream
- 1 teaspoon vanilla
- ½ teaspoon instant espresso powder (optional)

Nonstick cooking spray
Chocolate fudge ice cream topping
Crushed striped round peppermint candies (optional)

For peppermint ice cream, in a large bowl combine vanilla ice cream and ½ cup crushed peppermint candies. Stir with a wooden spoon until combined. Cover and freeze about 8 hours or until firm.

For the waffles, in a small saucepan combine butter and chopped unsweetened chocolate. Stir over low heat until melted and smooth; set aside to cool slightly.

In a medium bowl combine flour, cocoa powder, baking powder, baking soda, and salt; make a well in the center. In another medium bowl beat eggs slightly. Stir in sugar, half-and-half, vanilla, espresso powder (if using), and melted chocolate mixture. Add egg mixture all at once to the flour mixture. Stir just until moistened (batter should be slightly lumpy).

Spoon a scant ½ cup batter onto grids of a preheated, lightly greased 7½-inch round waffle maker. Close lid quickly; do not open until done. Bake about 1 minute or until waffles are cooked through. (Waffles will not be crisp; do not overcook.) Carefully transfer to a wire rack to cool. Repeat with remaining batter.

Separate waffles into quarters. Arrange waffle sections and ice cream in serving bowls. Drizzle with ice cream topping and sprinkle with additional crushed peppermint candies, if desired. Makes about 10 servings.

TIP: Waffles may be made ahead. Store baked and cooled waffles in an airtight container at room temperature up to 24 hours. Freeze for longer storage.

Tasty Bran Waffles

88

Tasty Bran Waffles

✳

Everyone will love these nutty-tasting delights at breakfast or brunch. They're also hearty enough to stand in for supper—especially if you serve them alongside chubby links of Polish sausage.

2 egg whites
1 cup all-purpose flour
¼ cup sugar
1 teaspoon baking powder
½ teaspoon baking soda
¼ teaspoon salt
1 cup buttermilk or sour milk*
2 egg yolks, beaten
1 cup whole bran cereal
6 tablespoons butter or
    margarine, melted
    Butter
    Syrup

Allow egg whites to stand at room temperature for 30 minutes. In a mixing bowl sift together the flour, sugar, baking powder, baking soda, and salt; set aside.

In a large mixing bowl beat egg whites with an electric mixer on medium to high speed until stiff peaks form (tips stand straight).

Stir the buttermilk and beaten egg yolks into the flour mixture. Fold in the cereal, melted butter, and egg whites. Pour batter onto grids of a preheated, lightly greased waffle maker. (Check manufacturer's directions for amount of batter to use.) Close lid quickly; do not open during baking. Bake according to manufacturer's directions. Repeat with remaining batter. Serve with butter and syrup. Makes 8 (4-inch) waffles.

***NOTE:** To make 1 cup sour milk, place 1 tablespoon lemon juice or vinegar in a glass measuring cup. Add enough milk to make 1 cup total liquid; stir. Let mixture stand at room temperature for 5 minutes before using.

Overnight Three-Grain Waffles

✳

These waffles taste like fancy bed-and-breakfast fare. Overnight guests will love them—and you'll appreciate that they can be mixed the night before and baked in the morning. Also enjoy them after a busy day of shopping—stir them together before you head out the door.

1¼ cups all-purpose flour
1 cup yellow cornmeal
½ cup oat bran
3 tablespoons sugar
1 package active dry yeast
½ teaspoon salt
2 cups milk
2 eggs
⅓ cup cooking oil
    Praline Sauce (see below) or
      maple syrup

In a large mixing bowl combine the flour, cornmeal, oat bran, sugar, yeast, and salt. Add the milk, eggs, and oil; beat with a rotary beater or an electric mixer for 1 minute on medium speed until thoroughly combined. Cover loosely and let stand for 1 hour at room temperature or for 2 to 24 hours in the refrigerator until mixture is bubbly and slightly thickened.

Meanwhile, prepare Praline Sauce. Stir batter. Pour batter onto a preheated, lightly greased waffle maker. (Check manufacturer's directions for amount of batter to use.) Close lid quickly; do not open during baking. Bake according to manufacturer's directions. Use a fork to remove baked waffle from grid; keep hot. Repeat with remaining batter. Serve immediately with Praline Sauce or maple syrup. Makes 8 (4-inch) waffles.

PRALINE SAUCE: In a small saucepan combine ¾ cup granulated sugar, ¾ cup packed brown sugar, and ½ cup half-and-half or light cream. Cook and stir over medium-high heat until boiling, stirring constantly to dissolve sugars. Boil, uncovered, for 1 minute. Remove from heat. Stir in ⅓ cup coarsely chopped pecans, 1 tablespoon butter or margarine, and ½ teaspoon vanilla. Stir sauce until butter melts. Makes 1½ cups sauce.

Oatmeal Waffles

*Spicy Molasses
Waffle Squares*

Oatmeal Waffles

✳

*Serve these filling waffles at breakfast or
brunch along with a big bowl of in-season
fresh fruit.*

1½ cups all-purpose flour
3 tablespoons packed brown
    sugar
2 teaspoons baking powder
½ teaspoon ground cinnamon
¼ teaspoon salt
1 cup quick-cooking rolled oats
2 eggs
1½ cups milk
⅓ cup cooking oil
   Powdered sugar (optional)
   Maple syrup (optional)
   Fresh fruit (optional)
   Vanilla yogurt (optional)

In a large bowl stir together flour,
brown sugar, baking powder, cinnamon,
and salt. Stir in oats. Make a well in the
center of flour mixture; set aside.
In a medium bowl beat eggs slightly.
Stir in milk and oil. Add egg mixture
all at once to flour mixture; stir
until combined.

Pour a generous cup of batter onto
grid of a preheated, lightly greased
waffle maker. Close lid quickly; do not
open during baking. Bake according to
manufacturer's directions. Use a fork to
lift baked waffle off grid. Repeat with
remaining batter. If desired, sprinkle
waffles with powdered sugar, serve with
maple syrup, or top with fruit and
yogurt. Makes 12 (4-inch) waffles.

Spicy Molasses
Waffle Squares

✳

*Molasses and spice cookies are a
Christmastime classic. Why not let your
waffle maker put a festive stamp on
goodies? They'll also work as a sweet
breakfast treat.*

⅔ cup all-purpose flour
½ cup whole wheat flour
½ cup packed brown sugar
½ teaspoon baking powder
¼ teaspoon salt
¼ teaspoon ground cinnamon
⅛ teaspoon ground ginger
   Dash ground cloves

2 slightly beaten eggs
¼ cup butter or margarine,
   melted
2 tablespoons molasses
   Orange Glaze (see below)

Lightly grease a waffle maker; preheat.
In a medium bowl stir together the
all-purpose flour, whole wheat flour,
brown sugar, baking powder, salt,
cinnamon, ginger, and cloves; set aside.
In another bowl combine eggs,
melted butter, and molasses. Add egg
mixture all at once to flour mixture. Stir
just until mixture is moistened.
Drop batter by rounded teaspoons
3 inches apart onto grid of waffle baker.
Bake 1 to 1½ minutes or until cookies
are golden brown. Use a fork to lift
cookies off grid.
Transfer cookies to wire rack to cool.
Repeat with remaining batter. Drizzle
cooled cookies with Orange Glaze.
Makes about 25 cookies.
ORANGE GLAZE: In a small bowl stir
together ¾ cup sifted powdered sugar
and ½ teaspoon finely shredded orange
peel. Stir in enough orange juice
(3 to 4 teaspoons) to make glaze of
drizzling consistency.

89

Pastel Cream Wafers

Better Homes and Gardens® magazine has published countless unforgettable Christmas cookie recipes. Here are 10 favorites—some timeless winners and some forgotten treasures that are due for a spirited revival.

eight decades of great cookies!

Pastel Cream Wafers

✳

Buttery sweet pastel frosting nestles between disks of light, flaky pastry for a lovely sandwich cookie that truly melts in your mouth.

- ½ cup cold butter (no substitutes)
- 1 cup all-purpose flour
- 3 to 4 tablespoons light cream or half-and-half
  Sanding sugar or granulated sugar
  Powdered Sugar Frosting
  (see right)

In a medium mixing bowl cut butter into flour until pieces are the size of small peas. Sprinkle 1 tablespoon of the cream over part of the mixture. Gently toss with a fork and push to side of bowl. Repeat until all is moistened. Form into a ball.

Roll dough on a lightly floured surface to slightly less than ⅛-inch thickness. Cut into rounds with a scalloped 1¾-inch round cookie cutter. Dip one side of each round in sugar. Place cutouts, sugared sides up, 1 inch apart on an ungreased cookie sheet. With a fork, prick four parallel rows in each cutout. Bake in a 375°F oven for 8 to 10 minutes or until edges just begin to brown. Transfer to wire racks to cool.

Spread a scant 1 teaspoon Powdered Sugar Frosting on the flat side of half of the cookies. Top with the remaining cookies, flat sides down. Makes about 20 sandwiches.

POWDERED SUGAR FROSTING: In a bowl stir together 1 cup sifted powdered sugar, 1 tablespoon softened butter (no substitutes), ½ teaspoon vanilla, 1 drop food coloring, and enough light cream or half-and-half (about 1 tablespoon) to make a spreadable frosting.

TO STORE: Place unfilled cutouts in layers separated by waxed paper in a covered, airtight container at room temperature up to 1 week or freeze up to 3 months. Fill just before serving.

Cherry-Coconut Drops

✳

Sometimes the best cookies are the easiest!

- 1 7-ounce package (2⅔ cups) flaked coconut
- 2 tablespoons cornstarch
- ½ cup sweetened condensed milk
- 1 teaspoon vanilla
- ½ cup chopped red and/or green candied cherries

In a medium bowl combine coconut and cornstarch. Stir in sweetened condensed milk and vanilla until mixture is combined. Stir in the chopped candied cherries. Drop by small rounded teaspoonfuls about 1 inch apart on a greased and floured cookie sheet.

Bake in a 325°F oven for 12 to 15 minutes or until lightly browned on bottoms. Cool on cookie sheet for 1 minute. Transfer cookies to a wire rack; cool. Makes about 24 cookies.

TO STORE: Place in layers separated by waxed paper in an airtight container; cover. Store at room temperature up to 3 days or freeze up to 1 month.

Cranberry-Orange Pinwheels

✳

These pretty pinwheel cookies roll up two great flavors of the season. Arrange the swirled goodies on a circular dish to give your presentation extra pizzazz.

    1 cup cranberries
    1 cup pecans
    ¼ cup packed brown sugar
    1 cup butter, softened
 1½ cups granulated sugar
    ½ teaspoon baking powder
    ½ teaspoon salt
    2 eggs
    2 teaspoons finely shredded
        orange peel
    3 cups all-purpose flour

For filling, in a blender container or food processor bowl combine cranberries, pecans, and brown sugar. Cover and blend or process until cranberries and nuts are finely chopped; set aside.

In a large mixing bowl beat butter with an electric mixer on medium speed for 30 seconds. Add granulated sugar, baking powder, and salt. Beat until combined, scraping sides of bowl occasionally. Beat in eggs and orange peel until combined. Beat in as much of the flour as you can with the mixer. Stir in any remaining flour with a wooden spoon. Cover and chill dough about 1 hour or until easy to handle.

Divide dough in half. Roll half of the dough between pieces of waxed paper into a 10-inch square. Spread half of the filling over the square of dough to within ½ inch of the edges. Carefully roll up dough, using the waxed paper to lift and guide the roll. Moisten edges; pinch to seal. Wrap in plastic wrap. Chill for 4 to 24 hours. Repeat with remaining dough and filling.

Cut rolls into ¼-inch slices. Place slices 2 inches apart on an ungreased

Cranberry-Orange Pinwheels

cookie sheet. Bake in a 375°F oven for 8 to 10 minutes or until edges are firm and bottoms are lightly browned. Cool on cookie sheet for 1 minute. Transfer cookies to a wire rack to cool. Makes about 60 cookies.

TO STORE: Place in layers separated by waxed paper in an airtight container; cover. Store at room temperature up to 3 days or freeze up to 3 months.

Blond Brownies

✳

In the past decade, "cookies in a jar" recipes have emerged as an easy, well-received homemade gift. The mix lets your gift recipients bake a batch of homemade cookies whenever they wish.

    ½ cup white baking pieces
    ¾ cup packed brown sugar
    2 cups packaged biscuit mix
    ½ cup chopped almonds, toasted
    ½ cup butter

    1 egg
    1 teaspoon vanilla

In a 1-quart glass jar or canister layer the following ingredients: white baking pieces, half the brown sugar, half the biscuit mix, remaining brown sugar, remaining biscuit mix, and almonds. Tap jar gently on the counter to settle each layer before adding the next. Cover jar and attach baking directions.

BAKING DIRECTIONS: Use mix within 1 month. Empty contents of jar into a large bowl. Add ½ cup butter, melted; 1 beaten egg; and 1 teaspoon vanilla. Stir until combined. Spread into a greased 8×8×2-inch baking pan. Bake in a 350°F oven about 25 minutes or until golden brown around edges and center is almost set. Cool in pan on a wire rack. Cut into bars. Makes 16 brownies.

92

Blond Brownies

Fry-Pan Cookies

Fry-Pan Cookies

✳

Here's an oldie but goodie—one of the best recipes from the days when cooks first discovered the wonders of using packaged cereal as a baking ingredient. If the mixture is sticky, lightly coat the scoop with nonstick cooking spray or dip it in water between scoops.

- 1 tablespoon butter
- 1/2 cup sugar
- 2 eggs, beaten
- 1 1/2 cups chopped pitted dates
- 1 teaspoon vanilla
- 2 1/2 cups crisp rice cereal
- 1/2 cup chopped nuts
- 3 cups flaked coconut

Melt the butter in a large skillet over low heat. In a small bowl stir together the sugar and the eggs. Add to skillet along with dates and vanilla. Cook and stir over low heat about 5 minutes or until thick. Remove from heat; stir in cereal and nuts.

Place coconut in a shallow dish. Using a cookie scoop or small ice cream scoop (No. 100 size, about 1 1/4-inch diameter), drop mixture into coconut; roll to coat. Refrigerate until firm. Makes 48 cookies.

To Store: Place in layers separated by waxed paper in a covered, airtight container. Refrigerate up to 1 week. Let cookies stand 30 minutes at room temperature before serving.

Coconut Diamonds

✳

This bar cookie took top honors in a Better Homes and Gardens Prize Tested Recipe contest in 1959 and continues as a favorite today!

- 6 tablespoons butter, softened
- 1/4 cup granulated sugar
- 1/4 teaspoon salt
- 1 cup sifted all-purpose flour
- 2 eggs
- 1 teaspoon vanilla
- 1 cup brown sugar
- 2 tablespoons all-purpose flour
- 1/4 teaspoon salt
- 1 cup flaked coconut
- 1/2 cup coarsely chopped walnuts

In a medium mixing bowl beat butter with an electric mixer on medium to high speed for 30 seconds. Add granulated sugar and 1/4 teaspoon salt; stir in 1 cup flour. Pat flour mixture onto the bottom of a 9×9×2-inch baking pan. Bake in a 350°F oven for 15 minutes or until lightly browned.

Meanwhile, in a medium mixing bowl beat eggs slightly with an electric mixer; add vanilla. Gradually add brown sugar, beat just until blended. Add the 2 tablespoons flour and 1/4 teaspoon salt. Stir in coconut and walnuts. Spread the brown sugar mixture over baked layer. Bake about 20 minutes more or until top appears set; cool. Cut into diamonds. Makes 18 cookie bars.

To Store: Place in an airtight container; store, covered, in the refrigerator.

Santa's Whiskers

Kris Kringles

Kris Kringles

✳

Orange and lemon peel add a zesty edge to these 1953 delicacies. Each cookie wears a bright cherry topknot—red or green for the holidays.

 ½ cup butter, softened
 ¼ cup sugar
 1 egg yolk
 1 teaspoon finely shredded
    lemon peel (set aside)
 1 teaspoon lemon juice
 1 cup all-purpose flour
 1 tablespoon finely shredded
    orange peel
    Dash salt
 1 slightly beaten egg white
 ⅔ cup finely chopped walnuts
 13 whole candied red or green
    cherries, halved

In a medium mixing bowl beat butter with an electric mixer on medium to high speed for 30 seconds. Add sugar; beat until combined. Beat in egg yolk and lemon juice until combined. Stir in flour, orange peel, salt, and lemon peel with a wooden spoon. Cover and chill dough for 1 hour or until easy to handle.

Shape dough into 1-inch balls. Dip balls in egg white; roll in chopped nuts. Place on a greased cookie sheet. Press a cherry half in the center of each. Bake in a 325°F oven for 20 minutes or until lightly browned. Transfer cookies to wire racks to cool. Makes about 26 cookies.

To Store: Place in layers separated by waxed paper in a covered, airtight container. Store at room temperature up to 3 days or freeze up to 3 months.

Santa's Whiskers

✳

In 1970, Better Homes and Gardens editors loved the way shreds of coconut resembled Santa's whiskers—the jolly little gems took top honors in that year's holiday cookie contest.

 ¾ cup butter, softened
 ¾ cup sugar
 1 tablespoon milk
 1 teaspoon vanilla
 2 cups all-purpose flour
 ¾ cup finely chopped candied red
    and/or green cherries
 ⅓ cup finely chopped pecans
 ¾ cup shredded coconut

In a large mixing bowl beat butter with an electric mixer on medium to high speed for 30 seconds. Add the sugar; beat until combined, scraping sides of bowl. Beat in milk and vanilla. Beat in as much of the flour as you can with the mixer. Stir in remaining flour, candied cherries, and pecans with a wooden spoon.

Divide dough in half; shape each half into an 8-inch log. Roll each log in coconut. Wrap each log in plastic wrap or waxed paper; chill for 2 to 24 hours.

Cut logs crosswise into ¼-inch slices. Place slices 1 inch apart on an ungreased cookie sheet. Bake in a 375°F oven for 8 to 10 minutes or until edges are golden brown. Transfer cookies to wire racks to cool. Makes about 60 cookies.

To Store: Place in layers separated by waxed paper in a covered, airtight container. Store at room temperature up to 3 days or freeze up to 3 months.

Crème de Menthe Brownies

✳

Crème de Menthe found its way into such recipes as mile-high chiffon pies and classic grasshopper cocktails. It has rarely tasted better, however, than in these beautiful chocolate bars. Pictured on page 56.

 ½ cup butter (no substitutes)
 2 ounces unsweetened
    chocolate, cut up
 1 cup granulated sugar
 2 eggs
 ¼ teaspoon mint extract
 ⅔ cup all-purpose flour
 ¼ cup butter (no substitutes)
 1½ cups sifted powdered sugar
 2 tablespoons green crème de
    menthe
 1 ounce semisweet chocolate
    (optional)
    Layered chocolate-mint candies,
    chopped or peeled into curls
    (optional)

Place the ½ cup butter and unsweetened chocolate in a heavy medium saucepan. Melt over low heat. Remove from heat. Stir in granulated sugar, eggs, and mint extract. Beat lightly by hand until just combined. Stir in flour. Spread batter in a 9×9×2-inch baking pan. Bake in a 375°F oven for 20 minutes. Cool completely in pan on a wire rack.

For frosting, in a medium mixing bowl beat the ¼ cup butter with an electric mixer on low to medium speed until fluffy. Gradually add 1 cup of the powdered sugar. Beat in crème de menthe. Gradually beat in remaining ½ cup powdered sugar to make of spreading consistency.

Spread crème de menthe mixture on brownies. If desired, melt semisweet chocolate in a small heavy saucepan over low heat. Drizzle chocolate over brownies. If desired, immediately sprinkle with chocolate-mint candies. Cut into triangles or bars. Makes 16 to 20 bars.

To Store: Cover and store in refrigerator up to 3 days; or freeze plain brownies up to 3 months. Thaw, then spread with crème de menthe frosting.

Sachertorte Cookies

✳

Over the years, Better Homes and Gardens editors have become experts at parlaying the flavors of celebrated desserts into easy-to-make cookies. This one is modeled after the Sachertorte, a famous Viennese chocolate-and-apricot torte.

    2 cups all-purpose flour
  ⅓ cup unsweetened cocoa
          powder
    1 teaspoon baking powder
  ¼ teaspoon baking soda
  ¼ teaspoon salt
  ¼ cup butter, softened
  ¼ cup cooking oil
    1 cup packed brown sugar
  ⅓ cup granulated sugar
    2 ounces unsweetened
          chocolate, melted
          and cooled
    1 teaspoon vanilla
    3 eggs
    1 8-ounce carton dairy
          sour cream
  ½ cup apricot preserves
          Chocolate Frosting
          (see right)
    1 cup milk chocolate pieces
    1 teaspoon shortening

In a bowl combine flour, cocoa powder, baking powder, baking soda, and salt; set aside flour mixture.

In a large mixing bowl beat butter with an electric mixer on medium speed for 30 seconds. Add oil, brown sugar, granulated sugar, unsweetened

Sachertorte Cookies

95

chocolate, and vanilla. Beat until combined, scraping sides of bowl occasionally. Add eggs one at a time, beating well after each addition. Beat in sour cream until combined. Beat in as much of the flour mixture as you can with the mixer. Stir in any remaining flour mixture with a wooden spoon.

Drop dough by rounded teaspoons 2 inches apart onto a large greased cookie sheet. Bake in a 375°F oven for 8 to 10 minutes or until tops spring back when pressed lightly. Transfer cookies to a wire rack to cool.

In a small heavy saucepan melt apricot preserves over low heat. Force preserves through a strainer with the back of a wooden spoon, discarding any large pieces. Brush tops of cooled cookies with strained preserves. Frost with Chocolate Frosting; let frosting dry.

To decorate cookies, in a small heavy saucepan melt milk chocolate pieces and shortening over low heat. Pipe or

drizzle a letter S on each cookie; let stand until set. Makes about 60 cookies.

CHOCOLATE FROSTING: In a small heavy saucepan melt 8 ounces semisweet chocolate and 2 tablespoons butter over low heat, stirring frequently. Remove from heat; stir in 2 tablespoons light-colored corn syrup and 2 tablespoons milk. Whisk until smooth.

To Store: Place cookies in layers separated by waxed paper in an airtight container; cover. Store in the refrigerator up to 3 days or freeze cookies (before brushing with preserves) up to 3 months. Thaw frozen cookies; brush with preserves, frost, and decorate.

Candy-Peanut Ice
Cream Cake
(see recipe page 101)

96

a new year's eve party with the kids!

You want to see your friends and you want to enjoy time with your family too. Why not combine the best of both and invite everyone over for the evening? Here's all the inspiration you need to celebrate a memorable New Year's Eve—clever invitations, a fun craft activity, and a terrifically tasty menu that appeals to guests of all ages.

As the New Year begins
And the old one ends
We'd love to celebrate
With our family and friends

Help us ring in 2005 at our

New Year's Eve Party

Friday, December 31, 2004
Beginning at 8:00 p.m.

Bob and Joan Patton
213 Waverly Avenue
West Des Moines, IA 50266

Please RSVP by Dec. 17, 2004
(515) 555-4...

Time with family is precious—and so is time with friends. Knowing that finding child care on New Year's Eve is nearly impossible, your friends will love it when you say, "Come on over—and bring the kids."

Inviting youngsters doesn't mean your party has to be about only the kids. Because New Year's Eve is generally an adult holiday, tap into the allure by adding a few adult touches. Set out festive plates and bowls, serve favorite foods, light candles, and play your generation's favorite music. For many children, there's something thrilling and memorable about being invited into the world of a grown-up party.

To stir excitement about the event, make and send beautiful handmade invitations. At the party, mix and involve your guests by asking them to make personalized wine charms that they can use and take home with them. At the stroke of midnight (or earlier if need be!), youngsters will feel oh-so special as they sip bubbling Shirley Temples

from elegant stemmed glasses ringed with their own handcrafted creations.

Just for this special occasion, we've assembled a best-of-both-worlds menu. Children will revel in a pasta dish that is, at its heart, based on kid-friendly mac-and-cheese. And the tasty, fun foods they can choose for pretty toppers make it unmistakably festive. Adults will feel indulged with a rich, opulent pasta made extra flavorful with porcini

mushrooms. For the utmost convenience, both dishes can start with the same pasta, if you wish.

For the finale, a beautifully big ice cream cake is an all-out showstopper, designed with everyone in mind. Use these recipes and ideas—along with a complement of your own fine touches—to make a fun and warm connection between kids and grown-ups this New Year's Eve.

Antipasto Kabobs

*Caramelized
Onion and Fig
Bruschetta*

98

Caramelized Onion
and Fig Bruschetta

✳

*This worldly appetizer was made with
adults in mind. Have the ingredients
ready to assemble just before the party,
then assemble and pop them into the
oven while the first refreshments are
being served.*

- 12 ½-inch slices baguette-style
French bread*
- 1 tablespoon olive oil
- 1 tablespoon butter
- 1 cup thinly sliced onion
- 1 ounce prosciutto, chopped
- 2 to 3 tablespoons fig preserves
- 2 to 3 ounces sliced Taleggio
cheese

Lightly brush both sides of each bread
slice with olive oil. Arrange bread slices
on an ungreased baking sheet. Bake in
a 425°F oven for 7 to 9 minutes or until
crisp and light brown, turning once. If
desired, transfer cooled toasts to a
storage container. Cover and store at
room temperature for up to 24 hours.
For caramelized onions, in a small
skillet melt butter. Add onions. Cook,
uncovered, over medium-low heat for
10 to 15 minutes or until onion is
tender and golden, stirring occasionally.
Remove from heat. Stir in prosciutto.
To assemble, spread fig preserves on
one side of toasted bread slices; top
with cheese and onion mixture. Return
slices to ungreased baking sheet. Bake
in a 425°F oven for about 3 minutes or
until heated through and cheese is
softened. Serve warm or at room
temperature. Makes 12 toasts.
*NOTE: If calling on the make-ahead
option in the first step, it's best to use a
softer variety of baguette-style bread.

Antipasto Kabobs

✳

*Go ahead—play with your food! Skewer
any combination of ingredients that will
be a hit with the kids in your crowd.
(Hint: Fruit and cheese usually rank
high.) Also design some skewers for more
sophisticated palates using olives and
imported meats.*

- 6 ounces sliced salami
- 6 ounces mozzarella or provolone
cheese, cubed
- 1½ cups cantaloupe and/or
honeydew melon balls
- 1 cup purchased large pitted
herbed green olives* and/or
large pitted ripe olives
- ¾ cup cherry tomatoes

On six bamboo skewers alternately
thread salami, cheese, and melon balls.
On another six skewers thread salami,
cheese, olives, and cherry tomatoes.
Place on a serving plate. Cover and chill
up to 2 hours before serving. Makes
12 kabobs (2 per serving).
*NOTE: Herbed green olives can be
found in Italian markets. However, if
you want to make your own, here's how:
In a small bowl combine 1 cup large
pitted green olives, pimiento-stuffed
olives, and/or pitted ripe olives;
1½ teaspoons olive oil; 1 clove garlic,
minced; ½ teaspoon dried Italian
seasoning, crushed; and ⅛ teaspoon
crushed red pepper. Stir until olives are
evenly coated. Cover and chill for at
least 2 hours.

Chicken and Wild Mushroom Pasta

✳

Inviting kids to the party doesn't mean the adults have to settle for a kids' menu! Treat yourselves to a rich, beautiful dish reminiscent of one you'd find at an upscale New Italian restaurant.

- 1 ounce dried porcini mushrooms
- 12 ounces dried penne pasta (3½ cups)
- 4 ounces prosciutto, finely chopped (¾ cup)
- 2 shallots, finely chopped (¼ cup)
- 2 cloves garlic, minced
- 2 tablespoons butter
- 2 cups whipping cream
- ½ teaspoon salt
- ¼ teaspoon freshly ground black pepper
- 1 6-ounce package refrigerated or frozen cooked Italian-flavor chicken breast strips
- ⅔ cup finely shredded Parmesan cheese
- 6 Roma tomatoes, peeled, seeded, and chopped
- ⅓ cup fresh basil chiffonade*

Rinse and drain dried mushrooms. In a small bowl soak the mushrooms for 20 to 30 minutes in enough warm water to cover. Drain mushrooms; discard liquid. Coarsely chop mushrooms; set aside.

In a Dutch oven cook pasta according to package directions; drain. Return pasta to Dutch oven; keep warm.

Meanwhile, in a large skillet cook prosciutto, shallots, and garlic in hot butter until shallots are tender but not brown. Stir in whipping cream, salt, and pepper. Boil gently, uncovered, about 3 minutes or until mixture thickens slightly. Stir in chicken and reserved mushrooms; heat through. Add chicken mixture and Parmesan to pasta, tossing lightly to coat. Heat through.

To serve, divide pasta mixture evenly among warm pasta bowls. Sprinkle with chopped tomato and fresh basil. Serve immediately. Makes 6 servings.

Chicken and Wild Mushroom Pasta

NOTE: In culinary terms, chiffonade refers to narrow strips of fresh herbs or lettuce. It is not only cut in such a way to look attractive, but it also helps release flavor. To make a chiffonade, stack the fresh basil leaves. Starting at a long edge of the stack, roll up the leaves. With a small, sharp knife, slice the roll into narrow strips, about ⅛ inch or narrower.

Fresh Greens and Winter Fruit Salad

✳

Salads are sometimes a hard sell for kids, but when you serve one that involves juicy ripe pears and colorful sweet red cherries, chances are they'll give it a thumbs-up! The adults, of course, will love it.

- 3 tablespoons olive oil
- 3 tablespoons champagne vinegar or white wine vinegar
- 1 teaspoon sugar
- ¼ teaspoon salt
- ⅛ teaspoon freshly ground black pepper
- 8 cups torn mixed greens
- 2 pears, cored and thinly sliced (1 cup)
- 1 small onion, very thinly sliced and separated into rings (optional)
- ⅔ cup pitted whole dates, snipped, or dried cherries
- ½ cup packaged glazed walnuts, chopped, or honey roasted sliced almonds
- 2 ounces Pecorino Romano or other firm-texture sheep's milk cheese, shaved

For dressing, in a screw-top jar combine oil, vinegar, sugar, salt, and pepper. Cover and shake well.

In a very large salad bowl combine greens; pears; onion, if desired; dates; and walnuts. Drizzle with dressing, tossing lightly to coat.

Divide salad mixture evenly among salad plates. Top with cheese shavings. Serve immediately. Makes 6 servings.

Cheesy Chicken and Pasta with Colorful Confetti

Pine Nut and Herb Twirled Breadsticks

100

Pine Nut and Herb Twirled Breadsticks

✳

These playful shaped wands will be a hit with kids and adults. To get a head start, prepare them just up to the baking step and refrigerate them up to 2 hours. Continue as directed.

- 12 10- to 12-inch bamboo skewers or wooden chopsticks
- ⅓ cup very finely chopped pine nuts
- ⅓ cup grated Parmesan cheese
- ¼ cup butter, melted
- 2 teaspoons dried Italian seasoning, crushed
- ¼ teaspoon garlic powder
- ¼ teaspoon freshly ground black pepper
- 1 11-ounce package refrigerated breadsticks (12)

Grease skewers or chopsticks. In a small bowl stir together pine nuts and cheese. Evenly spread pine nut mixture on waxed paper. In a small bowl stir together melted butter, Italian seasoning, garlic powder, and pepper.

Unroll dough and separate into strips. Stretch and twist each strip of dough around a greased wooden skewer to within ½ inch of each end. Generously brush each dough strip with butter mixture to coat. Roll in pine nut mixture. Place sticks on an extra-large lightly greased baking sheet, pressing under ends of dough to secure.

Bake in a 350°F oven for 13 to 15 minutes or until golden brown. Immediately remove from baking sheet and transfer to a wire rack. Cool for 1 to 2 minutes. Remove skewers. Serve warm. Makes 12 breadsticks.

Cheesy Chicken and Pasta with Colorful Confetti

✳

When hosting a house full of kids, this recipe will make everyone happy. Start with a big crowd-pleasing bowl of chicken and cheese pasta—then let them add the toppers they like to their servings.

- 1 pound dried shaped pasta
- ¼ cup butter
- 1 clove garlic, minced
- ¼ cup all-purpose flour
- 2 cups whole milk
- ½ cup sparkling apple juice or apple juice
- 8 ounces American cheese, shredded (2 cups)
- ½ cup freshly shredded Parmesan cheese
- 1½ cups chopped, cooked chicken Colorful Confetti (see right)

Cook pasta according to package directions. Drain and keep warm.

Meanwhile, in a medium saucepan melt butter. Add garlic; cook and stir for 30 seconds. Stir in flour. Stir in milk. Cook and stir over medium heat until thickened and bubbly. Stir in juice. Reduce heat to low; stir in cheese until melted. Stir in chicken; heat through. Pour sauce over pasta, tossing to coat.

Serve pasta with Colorful Confetti. Makes 6 servings.

COLORFUL CONFETTI: In small serving-size bowls place finely diced prosciutto or cooked ham, finely diced green sweet pepper, finely diced seeded Roma tomatoes, finely chopped pitted ripe olives, and freshly shredded Parmesan cheese. Cover and chill until ready to serve.

*Candy-Peanut
Ice Cream Cake*

Candy-Peanut Ice Cream Cake

✳

*Watch heads turn and smiles widen when
you bring this tempting cake to the table.
Decorate the top with any colorful candy
you wish—as long as it's festive!*

- 2 cups finely crushed chocolate
     wafers
- ½ cup melted butter
- ¼ cup sugar
- 1¼ cups coarsely chopped
     peanuts
- 4 cups vanilla ice cream (1 quart)
- 4 cups chocolate ice cream
     (1 quart)
- 1½ cups candy-coated chocolate-
     covered peanuts or other
     colorful candy

In a medium bowl combine chocolate
wafers, butter, and sugar. Press onto the
bottom and 2 inches up the sides of a
9×3-inch springform pan. Bake in a
350°F oven for 8 to 10 minutes or until
crust is set. Cool on a wire rack for
15 minutes. Cover bottom of crust with
peanuts; freeze for 40 minutes.

In a large bowl, using a wooden
spoon, stir the vanilla ice cream just
enough to soften. Spoon the softened
ice cream over peanuts in frozen crust,
spreading evenly. Freeze for 40 minutes
or until firm.

In a large bowl, using a wooden
spoon, stir the chocolate ice cream just
enough to soften. Spoon softened
chocolate ice cream evenly over vanilla
ice cream. Freeze for 40 minutes
or until firm. Top with candies,
pressing gently into the ice cream.
Cover and freeze for at least 4 hours
or up to 2 days.

Before serving, run a thin sharp knife
around the edge of the cake; remove
sides of pan. Let cake stand at room
temperature for 10 to 20 minutes to
soften slightly. To serve, cut into
wedges. Makes 12 servings.

Shirley Temples

✳

*At the stroke of midnight, bring out the
bubbly for everyone—including this
sparkling sipper for the younger set.*

- 1 10-ounce jar maraschino
     cherries with stems
     Ice
- 1 32-ounce bottle ginger ale or
     lemon-lime carbonated
     beverage, chilled
     Orange slices

Drain cherries, reserving juice (you
should have about ½ cup juice). Set
aside cherries. Fill 6 serving glasses with
ice. Divide cherry juice among glasses.
Divide ginger ale among glasses.
Garnish each serving with an orange
slice and a cherry. Reserve remaining
cherries for another recipe. Makes
6 (6-ounce) servings.

101

Shirley Temples
(instructions for glass
markers on page 103)

Set up a crafting table to keep the kids busy while adults socialize. Pre-cut the papers and have a few napkin rings, place cards, and stemware markers available as models. Then let the kids release their own imaginations.

102

What You'll Need...

- [ ] Vellum sheets
- [ ] Blue metallic paper
- [ ] Serpentine-patterned green metallic paper
- [ ] Copies of the New Year's paper on page 154
- [ ] Metal ruler
- [ ] 12-inch paper trimmer or scissors
- [ ] Double-sided tape
- [ ] 1/8-inch hole punch
- [ ] Silver mini-brads
- [ ] 3/8-inch-wide sheer ribbon
- [ ] Metal-edged star-shape vellum tags
- [ ] Large star-shape confetti
- [ ] Archival glue
- [ ] Bone folder or spoon
- [ ] Narrow-tipped black pigment marker

As the New Year begins
And the old one ends
We'd love to celebrate
With our family and friends

Help us ring in 2005 at our

New Year's Eve Party

Friday, December 31, 2004
Beginning at 8:00 p.m.

Bob and Joan Patton
2013 Waverly Avenue
West Des Moines, IA 50266

Please RSVP by Dec. 17, 2004
(515) 555-4023

Cocktails, Hors d'oeuvres & Dinner
Fun and games for children
Young and old

invitation

1 Print or hand-letter the invitation on the vellum. Let the ink dry completely.

2 Cut the papers as follows: blue, 5×7 inches; green, 4¾×6½ inches; patterned, 4½×6½ inches. Cut the vellum to the same size as the patterned paper, centering the verse.

3 Center the patterned paper over the green paper and join the two with tape. Lay the vellum over the patterned paper. Mark a point ¾ inch down from the top of the green paper and centered left to right. Punch a hole through all 3 layers at this mark.

4 To attach the vellum star, cut a 3-inch length of ribbon. Pinch the center of the ribbon together and slip it between the prongs of a brad. Slip the brad through the hole in the star and punched hole; fold the prongs back. Tie the ribbon in a knot and trim the ends.

5 Center the invitation on the blue paper backing and attach the backing with tape. Randomly glue three confetti stars to the vellum.

place cards

1 Cut the papers as follows: blue, 4x4 inches; green, 3¾x1¾ inches; patterned, 3½x1½ inches.

2 Trace each guest's name onto a vellum star, using computer type as a pattern. Names also can be handwritten.

3 Fold the blue paper in half to make the tent-shape place card base. Crease the fold with a bone folder or the back of a spoon. Center the green paper and then the patterned paper on one side of the place card. Tape the layers together.

4 Place the vellum star on the place card. Mark through the hole of the star onto the card. Punch through the mark. To attach the star, cut a 3-inch length of ribbon. Pinch the center of the ribbon together and slip it between the prongs of a brad. Slip the brad through the holes; fold the prongs back. Tie the ribbon in a knot and trim the ends.

5 Glue one confetti star to the vellum star and two to the patterned paper.

napkin rings

1 Cut the papers as follows: blue, 6¾x1½ inches; green, 6¾x1¼ inches; patterned, 6¾x1 inches. Cut a 6¾-inch-long piece of ribbon.

2 Trace 2005 or the appropriate year onto a vellum star, using computer type as a pattern. It also can be handwritten.

3 Layer the blue, green, and printed strips together, centering each paper on the previous one. Join the strips with double-sided tape. Center the ribbon over the printed paper and adhere on each end with tape.

4 Loop the papers into a circle so the ends overlap by approximately ½ inch. Punch a hole through all layers and join the ends with a brad and tape.

5 Place the vellum star on the napkin ring in the desired spot. Mark through the hole of the star onto the paper. Punch through the mark. To attach the vellum star, cut a 3-inch length of ribbon. Pinch the center of the ribbon

together and slip it between the prongs of a brad. Slip the brad through the hole in the star and punched hole; fold the prongs back. Tie the ribbon in a knot and trim the ends.

What You'll Need...

- ☐ Charms and buttons in kid-inspired designs
- ☐ Assorted beads
- ☐ Muffin tin or custard cups
- ☐ Beading loops
- ☐ Needle-nose pliers

glass markers

1 Separate the beads and buttons into muffin tins or custard cups. Straighten the end of large beading loops to make it easier to thread the beads and buttons onto the wire.

2 After the loops are at least partially full, use needle-nose pliers to bend the end of the wire back into place so it hooks into the loop on the other end and prevents the beads from sliding off.

103

Creamy Dutch Oven Chowder

autumn
soup party

Before the holiday season shifts into full gear, gather family and friends for a simple party that features robust, warming soups that everyone will love. The recipes also are perfect for easy-going get-togethers throughout the season.

Who doesn't love soup—especially on a crisp fall day or a snowy winter's eve? This season, host a gathering of friends and serve a big pot or two of soup as the centerpiece. It's a convivial, easy-on-the-cook way to entertain anytime.

Although the title of this story is "Autumn Soup Party," the concept works well throughout the season. Close to the holidays, gather friends for an ornament-making party. Choose a project from this book that everyone can craft together, and let each guest take home a decoration to cherish for years. Or reserve a night for relatives to visit and help trim your tree. Reward them for a job well done with this enticing menu.

Flag these recipes for a post-holiday party as well. If you had the best intentions of seeing certain friends around the holidays, but never managed to find the time, this menu is just as heartwarming in January or February.

Note that each soup makes six servings; serve both for variety, and you'll have plenty of soup for eight to ten guests (assuming many will want to taste both soups—and chances are, they will).

Creamy Dutch Oven Chowder

✳

If you serve this Christmas Eve, add the oysters, which are a holiday tradition for many families.

    4 slices bacon
    2 large carrots, sliced ½ inch thick
       (1½ cups)
    2 medium parsnips, sliced
       ½ inch thick, cutting larger
       pieces in half (1½ cups)
    2 medium onions, cut into thin
       wedges
    3 medium potatoes, chopped
       (3 cups)
    2 14-ounce cans reduced-sodium
       chicken broth
    ½ teaspoon garlic salt
    ¼ teaspoon black pepper
    3 tablespoons butter or margarine,
       melted
    3 tablespoons all-purpose flour
    2 cups milk
    2 cups frozen whole kernel corn
    1 pint shucked oysters with juice
       (optional)
       Snipped fresh chives or parsley
       (optional)

In a 4-quart Dutch oven cook bacon until crisp. Remove bacon, reserving 1 tablespoon drippings in the Dutch oven. Drain bacon on paper towels; crumble and set aside.

Add carrots, parsnips, and onions to Dutch oven. Cook over medium heat for 8 to 10 minutes or until brown, stirring occasionally.

Add potatoes, chicken broth, garlic salt, and pepper. Bring to boiling; reduce heat. Simmer, covered, about 15 minutes or until potatoes are tender. (At this point the mixture can be cooled, covered, and chilled in the refrigerator overnight.)

In a small bowl stir together melted butter and flour. Stir flour mixture, milk, and corn into vegetable mixture in Dutch oven. Cook and stir over medium heat until slightly thickened. If desired, add oysters and liquid to Dutch oven; cook until heated through and oysters curl around edges.

To serve, ladle chowder into bowls. Sprinkle each serving with crumbled bacon and, if desired, chives. Makes 8 to 10 side-dish servings or 6 main-dish servings.

Three-Cheese Spread with Almonds

✳

For a hearty appetizer spread, present this irresistible dip alongside a selection of imported meats, such as salami, mortadella, and prosciutto.

    1 8-ounce package cream cheese,
       softened
    1 8-ounce carton dairy sour cream
    1 cup shredded process Swiss
       cheese (4 ounces)
    2 ounces crumbled blue cheese
       (½ cup)
    1 tablespoon white wine
       Worcestershire sauce
    1 teaspoon paprika
    ½ cup chopped almonds, toasted
       Crackers and/or party rye bread

Beat together all ingredients except nuts and crackers until light and fluffy. Cover; chill up to 24 hours. Stir in nuts just before serving. Serve with crackers. Makes 2½ cups spread.

Checkerboard Rolls

Mixed Citrus Salad

Checkerboard Rolls

✳

This trio of tasty rolls is the perfect filler when served with soup or salad. Just prepare the different seasonings, and roll away!

    2 tablespoons poppy seeds
    2 tablespoons sesame seeds
    1 teaspoon lemon-pepper
       seasoning
    2 tablespoons yellow cornmeal
    2 tablespoons grated or finely
       shredded Parmesan cheese
    3 tablespoons butter, melted
    16 1.3-ounce pieces frozen white
       roll dough

In a shallow dish combine poppy seeds, sesame seeds, and lemon-pepper. In a second shallow dish combine cornmeal and Parmesan cheese. In a third dish place the melted butter. Working quickly, roll dough pieces in butter, then in one of the seasoning blends to lightly coat (half the rolls in one seasoning and the other half in the other seasoning).

In a greased 9-inch square baking pan alternate the rolls to resemble a checkerboard. Cover rolls with greased plastic wrap. Place covered rolls in refrigerator to thaw overnight.

Remove rolls from refrigerator; uncover and let stand at room temperature for 45 minutes.

Bake rolls in a 375°F oven for 15 to 20 minutes or until golden. Cool slightly on a wire rack. Serve warm. Makes 16 rolls.

SUNFLOWER-CUMIN TOPPER: Substitute 2 teaspoons coarsely crushed cumin seeds and 3 tablespoons shelled chopped sunflower seeds for one of the seasoning blends.

WHEAT GERM-CARAWAY TOPPER: Substitute 3 tablespoons toasted wheat germ and 2 to 3 teaspoons coarsely crushed caraway seeds for one of the seasoning blends.

Mixed Citrus Salad

✳

With colorful oranges and grapefruit, this salad adds beautiful sparkle to the table.

    2 pink or red grapefruit
    2 navel oranges
    4 cups thinly sliced Belgian endive
    4 cups torn escarole

    1 small jicama, peeled and cut into
       matchsticks (about 2 cups)
       Citrus-Dijon Dressing (see below)

Peel and section grapefruit and oranges over a bowl; reserve any juices.

Place greens on a large serving platter. Arrange fruit and jicama on greens. Drizzle Citrus-Dijon Dressing over salad. Serve immediately. Makes 10 servings.

CITRUS-DIJON DRESSING: Combine reserved fruit juices, ½ cup salad oil, 1 teaspoon lemon peel, ¼ cup lemon juice, 2 teaspoons sugar, 1 tablespoon Dijon-style mustard, and ¼ teaspoon freshly ground black pepper in a screw-top jar. Cover; shake well.

Italian Bean Soup

✳

You'll love this robust country-style soup on a cold night. If serving buffet style, place herb toasts on a tray beside the slow cooker for guests to top their own bowls of soup.

    1 cup dry Great Northern beans
    1 cup dry red beans or pinto beans
    5 cups cold water
    3 14-ounce cans vegetable broth

1 medium onion, chopped (½ cup)
2 cloves garlic, minced
2 teaspoons dried Italian seasoning, crushed
¼ teaspoon black pepper
1 14½-ounce can diced tomatoes with basil, oregano, and garlic, undrained
1 9-ounce package frozen Italian green beans or cut green beans
2 tablespoons balsamic vinegar
2 tablespoons butter, softened
¼ teaspoon garlic powder
¼ teaspoon dried Italian seasoning, crushed
12 ½-inch slices baguette-style French bread

Rinse beans. In a Dutch oven combine beans and cold water. Bring to boiling; reduce heat. Simmer, uncovered, for 10 minutes. Remove from heat. Cover and let stand for 1 hour. Drain and rinse beans.

In a 4- to 5-quart slow cooker combine beans, broth, onion, garlic, the 2 teaspoons Italian seasoning, and the pepper.

Cover and cook on low-heat setting for 10 to 12 hours or on high-heat setting for 5 to 6 hours or until beans are almost tender.

If using low-heat setting, turn to high-heat setting. Stir undrained tomatoes and frozen green beans into bean mixture. Cover and cook about 30 minutes more on high-heat setting or until beans are tender. Stir in balsamic vinegar.

Meanwhile, for the herb toasts, in a small bowl stir together butter, garlic powder, and the ¼ teaspoon Italian seasoning. Spread one side of each bread slice. Place bread on the unheated rack of a broiler pan or on a baking sheet. Broil 4 to 5 inches from the heat for 1 to 2 minutes or until crisp and light brown. To serve, ladle soup into bowls. Add 2 pieces of herb toast to each bowl of soup. Serve immediately. Makes 6 servings.

Ice Cream Cookies

✳

We decorated these delights with pretty fall-themed candy sprinkles. If you're serving these close to the holidays, use Christmas-themed sprinkles.

⅓ cup shortening
⅓ cup butter, softened
¾ cup sugar
⅓ cup unsweetened cocoa powder
1 teaspoon baking powder
1 egg
2 tablespoons milk
1 teaspoon vanilla
1⅓ cups all-purpose flour
½ gallon vanilla ice cream
Edible sprinkles
Chocolate and/or caramel ice cream topping (optional)

To make cookie dough, in a large mixing bowl beat shortening and butter for 30 seconds with an electric mixer on medium to high speed. Add sugar, cocoa powder, and baking powder; beat until combined. Beat in egg, milk, and vanilla until combined. Beat in as much flour as you can with the mixer. Using a wooden spoon, stir in any remaining flour. Divide dough in half. Cover; chill in refrigerator for 1 to 2 hours or until easy to handle.

On a lightly floured surface roll half the dough to slightly less than ¼-inch thickness. Using a 2½- to 3-inch round cutter, cut rolled dough into 24 to 30 shapes. Place shapes 1 inch apart on ungreased cookie sheets. Repeat with remaining dough.

Bake cookies in a 375°F oven for 7 to 9 minutes or until edges are firm and bottoms are light brown. Carefully transfer to wire racks; cool completely.

To prepare ice cream, line a 15×10×1-inch jelly roll pan with foil, using foil large enough to extend

Ice Cream Cookies

beyond two opposite edges of the pan. Place ice cream in a large chilled bowl. Using a wooden spoon, stir ice cream until softened. Using the spoon, transfer the ice cream to the foil-lined pan; spread evenly. Cover and freeze for 4 to 6 hours or until firm.

Use the foil to lift the ice cream from the pan. Using the same cookie cutter, cut out 12 to 15 ice cream rounds. Place leftover ice cream pieces in freezer bag or container for future use. Place each ice cream round between 2 cookies.

Place cookie sandwiches on a large cookie sheet; loosely cover and freeze until firm. Decorate edges with edible sprinkles. If desired, wrap each sandwich in freezer wrap and keep frozen for up to 1 month. To serve, place cookie sandwiches on serving plates and let stand 10 minutes before serving. If desired, drizzle with chocolate and/or caramel topping. Makes 12 to 15 cookie sandwiches.

109

Santa's Pear Pouches

Beginning in autumn and throughout the holidays, fresh produce aisles dazzle shoppers with fruits at their in-season best—pears, apples, oranges, cranberries, and an assortment of dried fruits. These are the bright flavors that star in this selection of sumptuous dessert recipes.

desserts of the season

Santa's Pear Pouches

✳

For a one-of-a-kind finale, serve these pretty pouches filled with luscious cardamom-infused pears and caramel topping.

3 medium red- or green-skin pears, cored and thinly sliced (about 3½ cups)
1 tablespoon sugar
1 tablespoon all-purpose flour
¼ teaspoon ground cardamom
⅓ cup butter, melted
8 sheets frozen phyllo dough (14×9-inch rectangles), thawed
¼ cup caramel ice cream topping
   Granulated sugar or coarse sugar
   Bay leaves (optional)*
   Fresh cranberries (optional)

For filling, in a medium bowl combine pears, 1 tablespoon sugar, flour, and cardamom. Toss to combine; set aside. **Brush four 6-ounce custard cups** with some of the melted butter; set aside. Place 1 sheet of the phyllo dough on a cutting board or other flat surface. (Keep remaining phyllo covered with plastic wrap to prevent it from drying out.) Lightly brush the phyllo sheet with some of the melted butter. Place another phyllo sheet on top; brush with butter. Repeat with two more phyllo sheets. Cut stack in half crosswise to form two 9×7-inch rectangles. Repeat with remaining phyllo sheets to make a total of four rectangles.

Gently ease one of the rectangles of stacked phyllo into the bottom and up the side of a custard cup (phyllo will hang over edge). Spoon about ¾ cup of the pear filling into center; drizzle

1 tablespoon of caramel topping over pears. Bring phyllo up over filling, pinching together to form a ruffled edge. (If desired, arrange 1 or 2 pear slices to poke through top of pouch.) Secure pouch with 100-percent-cotton kitchen string. Brush again with melted butter. Sprinkle with sugar. Repeat with remaining phyllo and filling. Place custard cups in a 15×10×1-inch baking pan.

Bake in a 375°F oven for about 20 minutes or until phyllo is golden brown. Cool 5 minutes in custard cups; remove from cups. If desired, tuck bay leaves under kitchen string and place a few cranberries on serving plate for garnish. Serve warm or cooled. Makes 4 servings.

***NOTE:** Bay leaves are for decorative purposes only in this recipe; remove them before serving and do not eat them.

To serve, loosen edges of custards with a knife, slipping the point of a knife down the sides to let in air. Invert a dessert plate over each custard; turn over cup and plate together. Scrape the caramelized sugar that remains in cup onto the custard. If desired, garnish with pomegranate seeds. Makes 8 servings.
*NOTE: Don't skip the water bath. It ensures the custards will cook slowly and evenly for smooth, silky results.

Thanksgiving Cake

✳

To toast coconut chips for this dreamy cake, spread them in a single layer in a shallow baking pan. Bake in a 350°F oven for 3 to 5 minutes or until light golden brown.

1¼ cups all-purpose flour
¾ teaspoon cream of tartar
¼ teaspoon baking soda
⅓ cup butter, softened
1 cup granulated sugar
¾ cup milk
4 egg whites
   Sifted powdered sugar
1 cup chopped hickory nuts, black walnuts, or pecans
¼ cup honey
2 teaspoons finely shredded lemon peel
1 cup snipped dried Calimyrna figs
   Snow-White Frosting
   (see opposite)
½ cup coconut chips, toasted

Grease a 15×10×1-inch baking pan; line pan with waxed paper. Grease and lightly flour paper; set aside. In a small bowl stir together flour, cream of tartar, and baking soda; set aside.

Pumpkin Crème Caramel

Pumpkin Crème Caramel

✳

The hallmark of American bistro chefs is the way they adapt classic dishes—such as crème caramel—with seasonal touches. This dessert taps into that trend.

1⅓ cups sugar
6 eggs, beaten
1½ cups canned pumpkin
2 5-ounce cans evaporated milk (1⅓ cups)
½ cup sugar
2 teaspoons pumpkin pie spice
2 teaspoons finely shredded orange peel
2 teaspoons vanilla
   Pomegranate seeds (optional)

To caramelize sugar, in a large heavy skillet melt the 1⅓ cups sugar over medium-high heat, shaking the skillet occasionally. When the sugar starts to melt, reduce heat to low. Cook, stirring frequently with a wooden spoon, until sugar is golden brown. Remove skillet from heat; immediately pour the caramelized sugar into eight ungreased 6-ounce custard cups. Holding cups with hot pads, quickly tilt to evenly coat bottoms of cups. Place cups in two 2-quart square baking dishes.

In a large bowl stir together eggs, pumpkin, evaporated milk, the ½ cup sugar, pumpkin pie spice, orange peel, and vanilla. Pour the pumpkin mixture over caramelized sugar in cups. Place the baking dishes on the oven rack. Pour boiling water into the baking dishes around cups to a depth of 1 inch*.

Bake in a 325°F oven for 40 to 45 minutes or until a knife inserted near the centers comes out clean. Carefully remove cups from water. Cool custards slightly on a wire rack. Cover and chill for 4 to 24 hours.

Thanksgiving Cake

In a medium mixing bowl beat butter with an electric mixer on medium speed for 30 seconds. Gradually beat in granulated sugar until well combined. Alternately add flour mixture and milk to butter mixture, beating on low speed after each addition just until combined.

Wash and dry beaters thoroughly. In a large mixing bowl beat egg whites with an electric mixer on medium speed until stiff peaks form (tips stand straight). Stir a small amount of egg whites into cake batter to lighten; fold batter into remaining egg whites.

Spread batter evenly into prepared pan. Bake in a 350°F oven for 12 to 15 minutes or until a wooden toothpick inserted near the center comes out clean. Loosen sides. Immediately invert cake onto a clean kitchen towel sprinkled with powdered sugar; remove pan and waxed paper. Cool cake completely. Cut cake crosswise into three 10×5-inch rectangles.

Meanwhile, in a small bowl combine nuts with 2 tablespoons of the honey and 1 teaspoon of the lemon peel. Set aside.

In another small bowl combine figs, remaining 2 tablespoons honey, and remaining 1 teaspoon lemon peel.

To assemble, place one cake rectangle on a platter. Spread nut mixture on cake layer. Carefully top with one-third of the frosting, allowing frosting to flow over edges. Top with second cake layer. Spread fig mixture on second cake layer. Carefully top with another third of the frosting. Top with third cake layer. Spread with remaining frosting, allowing it to flow over edges. Sprinkle top of cake with toasted coconut chips. Let stand 2 hours before serving; or cover and chill overnight. Makes 12 servings.

SNOW-WHITE FROSTING: In a large mixing bowl combine ⅓ cup pasteurized liquid egg whites or refrigerated or frozen egg product, thawed; 2 tablespoons lemon juice; 1 tablespoon honey; and 1 teaspoon vanilla. Gradually beat in 5 to 5½ cups sifted powdered sugar until frosting is a slightly flowing consistency.

Pumpkin-Pear Cake

✳

Recall how easy it is to make pineapple upside-down cake—and the wonderful taste of caramelized fruit. Here's a seasonal angle using pears and spiced pumpkin cake—for an unbelievably yummy dessert.

- ½ cup packed brown sugar
- ¼ cup butter, melted
- 1 teaspoon cornstarch
- 1 16-ounce can pear halves in light syrup
- 1½ cups all-purpose flour
- 1½ teaspoons pumpkin pie spice
- 1 teaspoon baking soda
- ¾ teaspoon baking powder
- 4 large egg whites
- 1 cup granulated sugar
- 1 cup canned pumpkin
- ½ cup cooking oil
  Sweetened whipped cream (see opposite) (optional)

In a small bowl combine brown sugar, melted butter, and cornstarch. Drain pears, reserving 3 tablespoons syrup. Stir reserved syrup into brown sugar mixture. Pour mixture into a 10×2-inch round baking pan or a 9×9×2-inch baking pan.

Cut pears into fans by making three or four lengthwise cuts from the bottom (wider end) of the pear to ½ inch from the top. Arrange pears, rounded sides down and small ends in the center, on the syrup in the pan.

In a small bowl combine flour, pumpkin pie spice, baking soda, and baking powder; set aside. In a large mixing bowl beat egg whites with an electric mixer on medium speed until soft peaks form. Gradually add granulated sugar, beating until stiff peaks form. Using low speed, beat in pumpkin and oil. Fold flour mixture into pumpkin mixture just until moistened. Carefully spoon batter over pears. Spread mixture evenly with the back of a spoon.

Bake in a 350°F oven for 40 to 45 minutes or until a toothpick inserted

Pear-Ginger Ice Cream

Pear Ice Cream

✳

For a pretty garnish, top each serving with a waffle-cone wedge dipped in melted white chocolate and coarse sugar.

- 2 ripe pears, peeled, cored, and chopped
- 3 tablespoons sugar
- 4 cups whole milk
- 1 1-inch piece fresh ginger, peeled and sliced
- 10 egg yolks
- 1¼ cups sugar

In a small bowl combine pears and the 3 tablespoons sugar. Cover; chill in refrigerator overnight. In a medium saucepan heat milk and ginger just until bubbles begin to form around pan edges.

In a large bowl whisk together egg yolks and the 1¼ cups sugar. Gradually whisk in the hot milk. Return all to saucepan. Cook and stir over medium heat until mixture just coats a metal spoon. Remove pan from heat. Quickly cool custard by placing the saucepan in a sink of ice water for 1 to 2 minutes, stirring constantly. Pour mixture through a strainer into a large bowl to remove ginger. Cover; chill in the refrigerator overnight.

Freeze custard mixture in a 4- or 5-quart ice cream freezer according to manufacturer's directions. Stir in pear mixture after ice cream has thickened. Ripen for 4 hours. Makes about 2 quarts or 16 (½-cup) servings.

near center comes out clean. Cool on wire rack for 5 minutes. Loosen from side of pan; invert onto serving platter. Serve warm with sweetened whipped cream, if desired. Makes 10 to 12 servings.

SWEETENED WHIPPED CREAM: In a small chilled mixing bowl combine 1 cup whipping cream, 1 to 2 tablespoons granulated sugar, and, if desired, 1 teaspoon vanilla. Beat with chilled beaters of an electric mixer on medium speed until soft peaks form. Do not overbeat. Makes 2 cups.

Lemon-Cranberry Pie

✳

Although lemon and cranberries may seem like too much pucker for a pie, sugar makes it perfectly sweet 'n' tart.

　　Pastry for lattice-top pie (at right)
1¼ to 1⅓ cups granulated sugar
　2 tablespoons all-purpose flour
　3 cups cranberries
　2 lemons, peeled (with white
　　　membrane removed), halved
　　　lengthwise, and thinly sliced
　1 egg white, beaten
　1 tablespoon water
　1 tablespoon coarse sugar

Prepare and roll out pastry. Line a 9-inch pie plate with pastry. Set aside.

For filling, in a large bowl combine granulated sugar and flour. Add cranberries and lemon slices; gently toss to coat. Transfer fruit mixture to pastry-lined pie plate. Top with a lattice crust. Trim pastry to edge of pie plate; crimp. Combine egg white and water; brush onto pastry. Sprinkle with coarse sugar. To prevent overbrowning, cover edge of pie with foil.

Bake in a 375°F oven for 25 minutes. Remove foil. Bake for 30 to 35 minutes more or until the top is golden and filling is bubbly. Cool slightly on a wire rack; serve warm. (Or cool completely on wire rack.)

Lemon-Cranberry Pie

Pastry for a Lattice-Top Pie

✳

A lattice topping is a quick way to add beautifully old-fashioned appeal to your pies.

　2 cups all-purpose flour
　½ teaspoon salt
　⅔ cup shortening
　6 to 7 tablespoons cold water

In a medium bowl stir together flour and salt. Using a pastry blender, cut in shortening until pieces are the size of small peas.

Sprinkle 1 tablespoon of the water over part of the flour mixture; gently toss with a fork. Push moistened dough to the side of the bowl. Repeat, using 1 tablespoon water at a time, until all the flour mixture is moistened. Divide dough in half. Form each half into a ball.

On a lightly floured surface, use your hands to slightly flatten 1 dough ball. Roll dough from center to edges into a 12-inch-diameter circle.

To transfer pastry, wrap it around the rolling pin; unroll pastry into a 9-inch pie plate. Ease pastry into pie plate, being careful not to stretch pastry. Fill pastry-lined pie plate. Trim pastry even with rim of pie plate.

Roll remaining dough into a circle about 12 inches in diameter. For lattice top, cut pastry into ½-inch-wide strips. Weave strips over the filling as desired. Press ends of strips into crust rim. Fold bottom pastry over strips. Seal and crimp edge. Makes 1 lattice-crust pastry.

Country Apple Tart

Country Apple Tart

✳

Dried figs—a favorite winter treat—combine with apricot preserves for a new flavor twist to an old-time favorite.

- 1½ cups all-purpose flour
- ¼ teaspoon salt
- ½ cup shortening
- 4 to 5 tablespoons cold water
- 4 cups sliced, peeled apples
- ½ cup snipped dried figs
- ⅔ cup apricot or peach preserves
  Milk
  Sugar

For tart pastry, in a medium bowl combine flour and salt. Using a pastry blender, cut in shortening until dough pieces are the size of peas. Sprinkle 1 tablespoon water over part of the mixture; gently toss with a fork. Push the moistened dough to side of bowl. Repeat with remaining water, using 1 tablespoon water at a time, until all the dough is moistened. Form dough into a ball.

Slightly flatten dough with your hands on a lightly floured surface. Roll dough from center to the edge into a 14-inch circle. Wrap pastry around rolling pin. Transfer to an ungreased baking sheet.

Arrange apple slices and figs in center of pastry, leaving a 2- to 3-inch border. Stir and evenly spoon preserves over fruit. Using your fingers, fold the pastry border up and over the filling, pleating the pastry to fit.

Brush the pastry border with milk and sprinkle it with sugar. Bake in a 375°F oven for 40 to 45 minutes or until fruit is tender. Cover loosely with foil during the last 10 to 15 minutes of baking, if necessary, to prevent overbrowning. Makes 8 to 10 servings.

Caramelized Oranges

✳

Following a generous holiday meal, these glistening ginger-kissed oranges and a tray of crisp meringue cookies purchased from the bakery will end dinner on a light, high-spirited note.

- 10 to 12 medium oranges or blood oranges
- 1½ cups sugar
- 1 cup freshly brewed hot tea
- 2 tablespoons finely snipped crystallized ginger
- ½ teaspoon vanilla
  Meringue cookies (optional)

Finely shred 1 teaspoon orange peel; set aside. Using a sharp knife, remove and discard the peel and white membrane from the oranges. Place the peeled oranges in a large bowl; set aside.

In a large heavy skillet heat the 1½ cups sugar over medium-high heat until sugar begins to melt, shaking skillet occasionally to heat evenly. Do not stir. Once sugar starts to melt, reduce heat to medium-low; cook for 5 to 6 minutes or until sugar is melted and turns a deep golden brown, stirring as needed with a wooden spoon. Do not overcook. Remove from heat.

Carefully and very slowly stir the hot tea into caramelized sugar. If necessary, return to heat; cook until any hard sugar particles dissolve. Cool. Stir in shredded orange peel, crystallized ginger, and vanilla. Spoon mixture over oranges in the bowl. Toss to coat. Cover and chill up to 24 hours. Stir again before serving.

To serve, slice each orange crosswise, then reassemble in serving-size dessert dishes. Divide syrup evenly among dishes. If desired, serve with meringue cookies. Makes 10 to 12 servings.

Pumpkin-Raisin Tart

Pumpkin-Raisin Tart

❋

Add holiday glitz to basic pumpkin pie with a rich layer of cream cheese, raisins, and nuts.

    Pastry for single-crust pie (right)
  1 8-ounce tub cream cheese
  ½ cup finely chopped pecans
  ⅓ cup raisins
  1 egg yolk
  2 tablespoons honey
  1 cup canned pumpkin
  1 5-ounce can evaporated milk
      (⅔ cup)
  ½ cup sugar
  1 egg white
  1 egg
  1½ teaspoons ground cinnamon
  ¼ teaspoon ground nutmeg
  ¼ teaspoon ground cloves
  ½ cup whipping cream
  1 tablespoon sugar (optional)
  2 tablespoons finely chopped pecans

Prepare pastry as directed; set aside. In a small bowl stir together cream cheese, the ½ cup chopped nuts, raisins, egg yolk, and honey; set aside. In a medium bowl combine pumpkin, evaporated milk, the ½ cup sugar, the egg white, whole egg, cinnamon, nutmeg, and cloves; set aside.

On a lightly floured surface roll pastry into a 13-inch circle. Ease pastry into an 11-inch tart pan. Press edges of pastry against edges of pan. Trim edges. Do not prick shell. Line the pastry shell with a double thickness of heavy foil. Bake pastry in a 450°F oven for 5 minutes. Remove foil. Bake for 5 to 7 minutes more or until pastry is nearly done. Remove from oven.

Reduce oven temperature to 375°F. Carefully spoon cream cheese mixture into baked pastry shell; spread evenly. Pour pumpkin mixture over cream cheese layer. Place tart pan on a baking sheet.

Bake tart for 30 to 35 minutes or until a knife inserted near the center comes out clean. Cool on a wire rack. Cover and chill for at least 2 hours or up to 2 days.

Before serving, in a medium mixing bowl beat whipping cream and, if desired, 1 tablespoon sugar with an electric mixer on medium speed until soft peaks form. To serve tart, remove outer rim of pan. Carefully lift tart from pan bottom with a large spatula; slide tart onto a serving platter. Spoon on whipped cream and sprinkle with 2 tablespoons chopped nuts. Makes 10 servings.

PASTRY FOR SINGLE-CRUST PIE: In a medium bowl stir together 1¼ cups all-purpose flour and ¼ teaspoon salt. Using a pastry blender, cut in ⅓ cup shortening until pieces are the size of peas. Sprinkle 1 tablespoon cold water over part of the flour mixture; gently toss with a fork. Push moistened dough to the side of the bowl. Repeat, using 1 tablespoon cold water at a time, until all dough is moistened (4 to 5 tablespoons total). Form dough into a ball.

Candied Candy Canes

easy recipes for

If you thought homemade candies were something only your grandmother had the time and talent to make, think again! With these simple recipes and tips, you'll transform basic ingredients into gorgeous food gifts that your family and friends will relish.

It's true—candy-making can be tricky. Forebears perfected the art through years of experience. They even had a mysterious vocabulary, using such phrases as "soft-ball stage" and "soft-crack stage" to determine that do-or-die point when their candies were ready to beat, pour, spread, or stretch.

With cooking terms as basic as "microwave" and "melt," the majority of the recipes here are much, much easier. Some recipes require little more work than melting chocolate or candy coating and dipping or sprinkling an ingredient into it. However, if you want to take candy-making to the next level, we'll show you how you can make a good old toffee or candy corn—even if you don't know a hard-ball from a soft-crack. (Hint: Use a candy thermometer.)

Candied Candy Canes

It's hard to believe that such a lovely, joyous candy can be made with just a few common ingredients.

    1 cup white baking pieces
    1 teaspoon shortening
   12 candy canes, about 5½ inches
       long
       Decorative red sugar,
       nonpareils, and sprinkles

In a saucepan combine baking pieces and shortening. Cook and stir over low heat until melted. (Or combine baking pieces and shortening in a microwave-safe bowl. Microwave on 70-percent power for 1 to 2 minutes or until baking pieces are melted, stirring every 30 seconds.)

Transfer melted baking pieces to a 1-cup glass liquid measuring cup. Dip the bottom or top half of each candy cane into the melted mixture, tilting cup to coat candy cane. Immediately sprinkle with or roll in decorative sugar, nonpareils, or sprinkles. Let stand for 1 hour or until coating is firm.

NOTE: If you have leftover melted candy coating, spread it on waxed paper and let it set. Chop the candy and sprinkle it on ice cream or stir it into cookie dough.

It's All in the Pan ...

The saucepan you use when making candy has much to do with the success or failure of your endeavor. Select a heavy-duty pan—and be sure to use the size pan specified. Many candy recipes specifically call for a 2-quart saucepan; in such cases, use one that measures 6 to 7 inches in diameter. Also, when preparing a recipe that calls for a candy thermometer, it's important that the pan you use has straight, not slanted, sides so the thermometer can clip on easily.

beautiful candies

Terrific Toffee

118

Terrific Toffee

✳

Surprise chocolate lovers on your gift list with this grand confection that features a triple hit of their favorite ingredient.

- 1 cup unblanched whole almonds, toasted and coarsely chopped
- ¾ cup semisweet chocolate pieces
- ¾ cup milk chocolate pieces
- ⅓ cup white baking pieces
- 2 tablespoons malted milk powder
- 1 cup butter
- 1 cup sugar
- 3 tablespoons water

Line a 13×9×2-inch baking pan with foil, extending foil over edges of pan. In a bowl combine almonds, semisweet and milk chocolate pieces, and white baking pieces. Sprinkle half (about 1½ cups) of the nut mixture on the bottom of prepared baking pan. Sprinkle malted milk powder on mixture in pan.

In a heavy 2-quart saucepan combine butter, sugar, and water. Cook over medium heat to boiling, stirring to dissolve sugar. Clip a candy thermometer to the pan. Cook, stirring frequently, until thermometer registers 290°F (soft-crack stage), about 15 minutes. Mixture should boil at a steady rate over the entire surface. (Adjust heat as necessary so that mixture does not boil over.)

Remove from heat; remove thermometer. Quickly pour sugar mixture over nut mixture in pan. Immediately sprinkle remaining nut mixture over toffee. Cool about 1 hour before breaking into pieces. If necessary, chill 15 minutes or until chocolate is firm. Makes about 2 pounds (36 servings).

Lemon Crunch Candy

✳

Studded with sprightly lemon-yellow candy bits, this treat adds a merry and bright appeal to holiday goodie baskets.

- 1 pound vanilla-flavored candy coating, cut up
- ¾ cup finely crushed hard lemon candies

Line a baking sheet with foil; set aside. In a heavy medium saucepan heat candy coating over low heat, stirring constantly until melted and smooth. Remove from heat. Stir in crushed candies, reserving some to sprinkle on top. Pour mixture onto the prepared baking sheet. Spread to about ⅜-inch thickness. Sprinkle with the reserved crushed candy pieces.

Chill candy about 30 minutes or until firm. (Or let candy stand at room

Lemon Crunch Candy

Simple Fudge

temperature several hours or until firm.) Use foil to lift firm candy from the baking sheet; carefully break into pieces. Store tightly covered for up to 2 weeks. Makes 1 pound candy.

Simple Fudge

✳

Old-time fudge recipes usually require beating the mixture by hand—up to 8 minutes. This recipe is so much creamier and easier!

1½ cups sugar
⅔ cup half-and-half or light cream
½ cup butter
2 cups tiny marshmallows or 14 large marshmallows
6 ounces 60% cocoa chocolate, chopped, or 6 ounces (1 cup) semisweet chocolate pieces

½ cup slivered almonds or chopped walnuts, toasted (optional)
1 teaspoon vanilla Cocoa powder (optional)

Line an 8×8×2-inch baking pan with foil, extending foil over edges of pan. Butter foil; set aside.

Butter sides of a heavy 2-quart saucepan. (A heavy 2-quart pan is important; otherwise the mixture will overcook and separate.) In saucepan combine sugar, half-and-half, and butter. Cook and stir over medium-high heat for 2 to 3 minutes or until mixture boils. Reduce heat to medium; continue cooking for 10 minutes, boiling at a steady slow rate and stirring constantly (mixture should not brown). Remove saucepan from heat. Add marshmallows, chocolate, nuts (if desired), and vanilla. Stir until marshmallows and chocolate melt and mixture is combined. Beat by hand for 1 minute.

Spread fudge evenly in the prepared pan. Score into squares while warm. Cover and chill for 3 to 4 hours or until firm. When firm, use foil to lift from pan. Cut fudge into squares; cut squares in half diagonally. Store tightly covered in the refrigerator up to 1 month. If desired, lightly sift cocoa powder over fudge before serving. Makes about 2 pounds (64 pieces).

Lining Pans with Foil

Some candy recipes, such as Simple Fudge, Terrific Toffee, and Almond Butter Crunch, instruct you to line a pan with foil. But how do you get that foil pushed into those corners without tearing it? Try this: Shape the foil around the outside of your pan, then lift it off and place it inside the pan, pressing it gently into the corners.

*Caramel Crunch
Corn*

120

Caramel Crunch Corn

✳

*Everyone who tastes this caramely, nutty,
buttery, crunchy homemade delight will
be thrilled. It's simply irresistible.*

 8 cups popped corn
 1 cup pecan halves, toasted
 1 cup slivered almonds, toasted
1⅓ cups sugar
 1 cup butter
 ½ cup light-colored corn syrup
 1 teaspoon vanilla

Remove all unpopped kernels from
popped popcorn. Place popcorn and
nuts in a 17×12×2-inch baking pan or a
roasting pan. Keep popcorn mixture
warm in a 300°F oven while making
the caramel mixture.

For the caramel mixture, butter sides
of a heavy medium saucepan; in
saucepan combine the sugar, butter,
and corn syrup. Cook and stir over
medium-high heat until mixture boils.
Clip a candy thermometer to the side of
the saucepan. Reduce heat to medium;
continue boiling at a moderate, steady
rate, stirring frequently, until the
thermometer registers 280°F (soft-crack
stage), about 15 minutes. Remove from
heat; stir in vanilla. Carefully pour
caramel mixture over popcorn mixture;
stir gently to coat. Spread popcorn
mixture on a large sheet of buttered foil
to cool. Quickly break into clusters with
two forks. Store in a tightly covered
container. Makes about 15 cups
(15 servings).

Candied Nuts

✳

*Present this treat in a beautiful cut-glass
dish for two gifts in one.*

1½ cups raw or roasted cashews,
  peanuts, whole almonds,
  and/or pecan halves
 ½ cup sugar
 2 tablespoons butter
 ½ teaspoon vanilla

Line a baking sheet with foil. Butter
the foil; set baking sheet aside. In a
heavy 10-inch skillet combine nuts,
sugar, butter, and vanilla. Spread evenly
in skillet. Cook over medium-high heat
until butter begins to melt. Gradually
stir melted butter into sugar until
combined (sugar will not be dissolved).
Reduce heat to low. Spread mixture
evenly in skillet. Continue cooking,
without stirring, until sugar begins to
melt. Cook and stir until sugar is golden
brown. Remove skillet from heat. Pour
nut mixture onto the prepared baking
sheet. Cool completely. Break into
clusters. Store tightly covered in the
refrigerator up to 3 weeks. Makes about
3 cups (12 servings).

Almond Butter
Crunch

✳

One of our best versions of toffee ever!

 1 cup butter
1⅓ cups sugar
 1 tablespoon light-colored corn
  syrup
 3 tablespoons water
 1 cup coarsely chopped blanched
  almonds, toasted
 7 2.6-ounce milk chocolate bars,
  melted
 1 cup finely chopped blanched
  almonds, toasted

**Line a 13×9×2-inch baking pan
with foil,** extending foil over the edges
of pan; set aside. Butter sides of a heavy

Two Secrets to Better Candy

Cooking candy at the proper rate and accurately determining when it is done are two critical steps to candy-making success. Here's help:

1. THE CANDY THERMOMETER
What's the No. 1 secret to foolproof toffee, caramel corn, and other candies that require boiling a mixture to a very specific temperature? Two words, one investment: candy thermometer. There's no better way to accurately test the stage of a hot candy mixture. Be sure to check the accuracy of the thermometer every time you use it. To test it, place the thermometer in a saucepan of boiling water for a few minutes, then read the temperature. If the thermometer reads above or below 212°F, add or subtract the same number of degrees from the temperatures specified in the recipe and cook and cool to those temperatures.

2. COOKING CANDY
Candy mixtures should boil at a moderate, steady rate over the entire surface. Our recipes suggest range-top temperatures. However, you may need to adjust the temperature of your range in order to maintain the best cooking rate and ensure candy will cook within the recommended time. Cooking too fast or slow makes candy too hard or soft. When stirring a hot candy mixture, use a wooden spoon.

Fruit and Hazelnut Clusters

2-quart saucepan. In saucepan melt butter; add the sugar, corn syrup, and water. Cook and stir over medium-high heat until mixture boils. Clip a candy thermometer to side of pan. Reduce heat to medium; continue boiling at a moderate, steady rate, stirring occasionally, until thermometer registers 290°F* (soft-crack stage), about 15 minutes. Quickly stir in almonds; spread in prepared pan.

Cool toffee about 2 minutes or until set. Spread half the chocolate on toffee; sprinkle with half the finely chopped nuts. Chill for 15 to 20 minutes or until chocolate is firm. Cover with waxed paper; invert onto a baking sheet. Spread with the remaining chocolate. Sprinkle remaining almonds on chocolate. Chill until chocolate is firm. Break into pieces. Makes 2¾ pounds (about 42 servings).

*NOTE: Watch carefully after temperature reaches 280°F.

Fruit and Hazelnut Clusters

✳

Steam the cranberries and toast the nuts for these festive little gems ahead of time—the candy will come together quickly. To keep the mixture from stiffening, place the pan of mixture in warm water while you fill the candy cups.

 1 cup dried cranberries
 1 cup golden raisins
 2 cups hazelnuts (filberts)
 1 pound vanilla- or chocolate-
      flavor candy coating, cut up

Place cranberries and raisins in a steamer basket. In a saucepan place the basket over, but not touching, boiling water. Cover and steam for 5 minutes. Remove fruits from steamer basket. Spread on paper towels and let stand at room temperature for 1 to 2 hours or until completely dry.

Meanwhile, spread nuts in a 15×10×1-inch baking pan. Bake in a 325°F oven for 15 minutes or until toasted. Rub warm nuts with a towel to remove skins. Cool for 20 minutes.

In a heavy large saucepan melt candy coating over low heat, stirring constantly. Remove from heat. Fold in hazelnuts and fruits. Drop mixture by teaspoonfuls into foil candy cups or onto waxed paper. Let candies stand in a cool, dry place for 30 minutes or until firm. Makes 60 candies.

◀ Peppery Cream Cheese with Nuts: Each ingredient needed for this instant appetizer has a long shelf life in the pantry or fridge. Keep them on hand and you'll always have festive nibbles to serve. Stir ¾ cup red or green jalapeño jelly until thinned. Place one 8-ounce package of softened cream cheese on a serving plate. Top with jelly; sprinkle with ¾ cup chopped toasted pecans. Serve with assorted crackers. Makes 16 servings.

In a Twinkling:
instant appetizers

▲ Pesto Roll-Ups: These festive bites add heartiness to appetizer spreads. To make them, separate one package of refrigerated crescent rolls into triangles; spread with purchased basil pesto. Cut each triangle in half, making 16 long triangles. Roll up triangles and place on an ungreased baking sheet. Bake in a 375°F oven for 12 to 15 minutes or until golden. Makes 16.

◀ Cucumber-Cheese Bites: Make these in 20 minutes and chill them up to four hours ahead. Spread a small amount of flavored cheese spread (such as boursin) onto ½-inch cucumber slices. Sprinkle with assorted toppers, such as snipped chives, crumbled bacon, finely chopped hard-cooked eggs, quartered cherry tomatoes, and/or sliced green onions.

◀ Marinated Antipasto Bowl: Layer just three ingredients—olives, marinated feta cheese cubes, and marinated artichoke hearts—in a stemware glass bowl. Use any combination of cheeses and olives that you like. You also can add chunks of imported Italian meats, such as salami, to the mix.

◀ Dried Cherry & Green Onion Spread: In a bowl combine 4 ounces softened cream cheese, ⅔ cup finely chopped dried red cherries, 3 tablespoons dairy sour cream, and 2 tablespoons finely chopped green onion. Spoon into pastry bag fitted with a 1¾-inch star tip. Pipe onto Belgian endive leaves. If desired, cover and chill spread up to 24 hours before piping. Makes 24.

▲ Prosciutto-Wrapped Fruit: Around the holidays, friends often send boxes and baskets of fruits as gifts. If you're lucky enough to be on the receiving end of this tradition, transform the bounty into appetizers. Simply wrap strips of very thinly sliced prosciutto around apple and/or pear slices. To prevent fruit from turning brown, brush with lemon juice before wrapping with the prosciutto.

▲ Nutty-Sweet Brie: You just can't go wrong with warmed Brie, especially when you can keep most of the ingredients on hand for drop-of-the-hat entertaining. To make, place an 8-ounce round of Brie in a shallow baking dish or pie plate. Bake in a 350°F oven for 10 minutes. Meanwhile, in a small saucepan combine ¼ cup butter or margarine; ¼ cup packed brown sugar, ¼ cup chopped nuts, and 1 tablespoon honey. Bring mixture to boiling over medium heat, stirring constantly. Pour sauce over Brie. Serve with crackers. Serves 8.

Lavender
Detergent
3/8 cup per load

124

giving from the heart

re recurring themes for busy families every year. Honor that desire with gifts that can be used well beyond the holiday season. Place mats, rugs, and patchwork clutches are appreciated again and again. Handmade package wraps and cards make the giving personal. Among this practical collection are a few pampering pleasures.

125

GIVING
from the HEART

make them in multiples

Set up the crafting table assembly-line fashion this year, making gifts for many friends all at one time.

snowman place mats & napkins

1 Wash and dry the place mats and napkins. Do not use fabric softener, dryer sheets, or detergents with additives. Iron all the pieces.

2 Apply the white paint to a corner of one place mat, creating three ball shapes for the snowman body. Extend small drifts of snow beyond the body. See the photograph *opposite* for details. Use a small brush to swirl and shape the paint, giving it a three-dimensional look. While the paint is still wet, sprinkle glitter over the surface. Let the paint dry completely, then shake off the excess glitter. Repeat for the other place mats. For interest, do some snowmen in pairs and alternate sides and figure placement. Paint a snowman in one corner of each napkin.

3 Dress each snowman to have a different personality. Glue seed beads to the face for eyes. Cut a tiny triangle of orange felt for the nose and glue it in place. Add ribbons for scarves. If desired, use more seed beads for buttons.

4 Using black paint, draw a black hat on each snowman, altering the shapes to fit their personality. Embellish the hats with dots of red and green paint, painted sprigs of holly, or other trims.

5 Add twig arms and hands using long stitches of perle cotton. Pull the knots to the back and secure the ends with a dot of glue.

What You'll Need...

- ☐ Purchased chambray place mat and napkins
- ☐ Metallic white dimensional fabric paint
- ☐ Small paintbrushes
- ☐ Super-fine white iridescent glitter
- ☐ Narrow red ribbon
- ☐ Black seed beads
- ☐ Orange felt scraps
- ☐ Fabric glue
- ☐ Black, red, and green dimensional paint
- ☐ Brown perle cotton

What You'll Need...

- Clear glass plate
- Photocopies or scans of the decorative holly papers on the inside covers of this book
- Matte-finish decoupage medium
- Disposable foam brushes
- Frosted spray paint for glass such as Krylon Frosted Glass Finish

decoupage plate

1 Wash and dry the plate completely, making sure there are no streaks or residue. Cut the paper to fit the flat portion of the bottom of the plate. Cut several individual holly motifs.

Paint the right side of the paper with a light coat of decoupage medium, covering the entire surface.

3 Using your fingers, smooth the right side of the paper onto the wrong side of the plate. Working from the center out, smooth out wrinkles or bubbles. Paint several coats of decoupage medium over the paper, taking care not to get it onto the rim of the plate. Apply the individual motifs to the rim in the same manner, omitting the top coats.

4 Remove any decoupage medium from the rim. Following the manufacturer's directions, apply several light coats of frosted spray paint to the back of the plate. Let it dry completely.

What You'll Need...

- [ ] 1 yard of natural linen for the towels
- [ ] 1¼ yards of 1¼-inch-wide yellow-green ribbon or fabric
- [ ] 1 yard of Christmas green baby rickrack
- [ ] Red washable felt
- [ ] Paper-backed fusible transfer web
- [ ] Embroidery floss in red, bright gold, yellow-green, and to match the linen
- [ ] Embroidery needle

poinsettia towels

1 Wash and dry all the fabrics. Use a commercial color-catching sheet when washing the red felt.

2 To make each towel, cut an 18×28-inch piece of linen. Fray ½ inch on both short ends. If using fabric instead of ribbon, narrowly hem the long edges. Sew the rickrack down the middle of the ribbon. Cut the ribbon in half crosswise; reserve the other half for the second towel. Edgestitch the ribbon to the towel 3 inches up from one short end. Narrowly hem the sides of the towel.

3 Trace the flower pattern *right*. Fuse the transfer web to the back of the felt according to the manufacturer's directions. Trace and cut the flower from red felt and fuse it to the towel just above the green band and centered horizontally. Using red floss, whipstitch around all the flower edges.

4 Cover the center oval of the flower with gold French knots. Scatter a few yellow-green French knots in the center.

5 Using a single ply of linen-colored floss, outline the inner edges of the petals with a couching stitch by following the lines on the pattern.

129

TO NANA from tezz

130

To:JANE From: AUNT KIKI

Happy Holidays!

in the mail...

Whether you send packages across the country or load them in the car for a trip across the state, these wraps will arrive without crushed bows, slipped ribbons, and lost cards.

mailable wraps

❧ Brush up on those childhood skills of cutting, gluing, and drawing and give your packages a grown-up look with handmade wraps. We have even included a custom-designed alphabet on *page 156* to use for labeling your packages. Use these ideas as inspiration, then apply your own imagination and artistic talents. *From left to right, top to bottom:*

Reindeer Handler: Cut and glue a pear-shaped reindeer head and face to a package. To make antlers, paint a child's hands with acrylic paint and "stamp" the antlers in place.

To the Point: Cut triangular trees from decorative paper and glue them to the package, alternating the direction. Add painted, stamped, or cutout stars.

Doggone Cute: Using a cookie cutter, coloring book, or other pattern, cut a dog from plaid paper. Glue it to the package and add a plaid ribbon collar and plaid ribbons at the ends.

Mr. Snowman: Cut a snowman head and scarf from white paper, a nose from orange, and a hat from green. Use markers to make the face and scarf stripes. Fringe the ends of the scarf. Glue the pieces in place and outline them with a thin marker. Glue snowflakes to the box.

A Place for Lace: Glue a square doily around the package so one point comes to a front edge. Add a ribbon bow at the point of the doily.

Have a Ball: Glue three circles to the box, then top them with rectangular caps that have been crimped or creased with a bone folder. Add rickrack stripes and cords for hangers.

Tipsy Tree: Cut a triangular tree from green paper, then make random horizontal cuts across the tree with decorative scissors. Add eyelets to each piece. Glue the tree down in a whimsical shape. Add a trunk, star topper, and string-wrapped packages.

Pass the Envelope: Fold contrasting paper around the package, trimming it to a point in the front so it resembles an envelope. Glue it in place and add a flat-backed trim to the point.

floor it

Add bands of color to a plain shaggy bath rug or white painted floor cloth to create gifts that are sure to be used and appreciated.

What You'll Need...

- ☐ Purchased primed floor cloth or primed canvas cut to the desired size
- ☐ Utility knife and straightedge, rotary cutter and mat, or sharp scissors
- ☐ Low-tack painters' tape
- ☐ Acrylic paint in the desired colors
- ☐ Disposable paintbrushes
- ☐ Polyurethane
- ☐ Circle cutter

What You'll Need...

- ☐ Various widths of polyester grosgrain ribbon in two or more desired colors
- ☐ Wood-burning tool
- ☐ Scrap of glass
- ☐ Tightly woven cotton shag bath rug
- ☐ Crafts knife
- ☐ Crochet hook or similar dull-edged tool
- ☐ Fabric glue (optional)

rich with ribbon

1 Using the wood-burning tool and working on a piece of glass, cut the ribbon into 8-inch lengths. The tool will both cut and seal the ends, preventing raveling. See *page 17* for details on cutting with a wood-burning tool.

2 Determine the desired placement of the stripes. Working from the back, mark the stripe lines. For each ribbon tuft, cut two slits through the rug backing. Space the pairs of cuts close together and leave a small space between the pairs.

3 For each tuft, use a crochet hook to push a ribbon end through each slit. From the front, pull the ribbon ends so the ribbon fits tightly against the back. Repeat for all the stripes. If needed, secure any loose ribbons to the back of the rug with fabric glue.

paint it pretty

1 If the canvas is not already the desired size, cut it to size. *Note:* Primed canvas is available by the yard at most art and crafts supply stores. Primed floor cloths are made only in standard rug sizes and may be harder to find.

2 Paint the entire cloth with two or more coats of the lightest color. While the paint dries, draw your pattern onto paper or graph paper. The rug shown *above* has stripes varying from ¾ inch to 5 inches in width. Using painters' tape, mask off the stripes for the second color. Paint two or more coats for the second color; remove the tape. Repeat for the remaining colors, letting each coat dry completely. Seal the rug with two or three coats of polyurethane.

3 To cut the circles on the ends, use a circle cutter (available at crafts stores) and space the circles evenly. If the cutter does not leave clean edges, finish them with a utility knife.

Lavender
Detergent
3/8 cup per load

making scents

Pamper your friends with linens scented by detergent, spray, and sachets in refreshing fragrances.

What You'll Need...

- [ ] Water
- [ ] Essential oil
- [ ] Clean bottle with a cork or cap
- [ ] Colored wax or clear wax and wax coloring
- [ ] Tin can and saucepan or an old double boiler
- [ ] Hand-printed label
- [ ] Dried herb sprig

linen mist

1 Add approximately 10 drops of essential oil to every cup of water. Adjust the amount as desired. The scent should be strong but not overpowering.

2 Pour the scented water into the bottle and cap or cork it tightly. Place the wax and coloring in a tin can or the top of a double boiler. Place the can in a pan of water, making sure it does not rock or tip. Place the pan on the stove burner and melt the wax using a medium-low temperature. Do not leave the wax unattended and keep it away from open flames.

3 After the wax melts, remove it from the stove and let it cool slightly. Dip the top of the bottle into the wax to seal the cap or cork. Repeat to build up a good coating of wax. See the photograph on *page 136* for details.

4 Add a decorative label. If desired, hot-glue a sprig of dried herb to the label. To use the mist, pour it into a spray bottle and lightly spray bed linens, towels, or the air.

What You'll Need...

- Clear, unscented natural liquid laundry detergent such as Seventh Generation
- Essential oil
- Clean bottle with a cork or cap
- Colored wax or clear wax and wax coloring
- Tin can and saucepan or an old double boiler
- Hand-printed label
- Dried herb sprig or other bottle trims (optional)

What You'll Need...

- Polyester or nylon organza scrap
- Fade-out fabric marker
- Wood-burning tool
- Glass scrap (optional)
- Small funnel
- Dried lavender, lemon verbena, or other desired fragrant herb
- Ribbon

scented detergent

1 Add approximately 25 drops of essential oil to every 2 cups of detergent. Adjust the amount as desired. The scent should be strong but not overpowering.

2 Pour the detergent into the bottle and cap or cork it tightly. Place the wax and coloring in a tin can or the top of a double boiler. Place the can in a pan of water, making sure it does not rock or tip. Place the pan on the stove burner and melt the wax using a medium-low temperature. Do not leave the wax unattended and keep it away from open flames.

drawer sachets

1 Cut a 4×12-inch piece of organza and fold it in half lengthwise with right sides facing; pin the fabric in place. Draw a line on the long side 1 inch from the fold. Draw another line 1 inch from the bottom edge. Sew along the lines.

Run a heated wood-burning tool just outside the stitching line to seal the edges and trim away the excess fabric. See *page 17* for tips on using a wood-burning tool on fabric. Turn the sachet to the right side. Using a funnel, fill the sachet to within 1 inch of the top. Seal and trim the top using the wood-burning tool. Tie a ribbon above the top of the herbs. Place the sachet in the folds of stored bed linens or towels.

3 After the wax melts, remove it from the stove and let it cool slightly. Dip the top of the bottle into the wax to seal the cap or cork. Repeat to build up a good coating of wax.

4 Add a decorative hand-written label, including the amount of detergent to use per load of laundry. If desired, hot-glue a sprig of dried herb to the label and tie ribbon or wired silk boxwood garland around the neck for decoration.

What You'll Need...

- Polyester or nylon organza scrap
- Fade-out fabric marker
- Small funnel
- Dried lavender, lemon verbena, or other desired fragrant herbs
- Ribbon
- Wood-burning tool
- Glass scrap (optional)
- Fabric glue

pillow sachets

1 Cut two 5-inch-squares of organza. Lay one square over the other with wrong sides facing and pin them in place. Mark a 2½-inch square in the middle. Sew along the marked lines, leaving a small opening for filling the sachet.

What You'll Need...

- Purchased or self-made muslin bag, approximately 3×5 inches
- Dried lavender, lemon verbena, or other desired fragrant herb
- Needle and thread
- Ribbon

2 Add a small amount of dried herbs to the sachet and sew the opening closed.

dryer sachets

1 Fill the bag three-fourths full of lavender or other dried herbs. Take a small stitch in the side seam of the bag just above the top of the herbs. Wrap the thread very tightly around the bag several times, sealing it completely. Take several small stitches in the side seam of the bag to knot the thread. Clip the thread. Tie a ribbon over the thread. NOTE: Be sure to close the bag tightly. Loose herbs may stain fabrics. Each dryer sachet will scent approximately 15 to 20 loads of laundry.

3 Align one edge of the ribbon along the stitching line and draw a line along the other edge. Remove the ribbon. Run the heated wood-burning tool along this line to seal the edges and trim away the excess fabric. See *page 17* for tips on using a wood-burning tool on fabric.

4 Glue the ribbon to the sachet margin. Trim and seal the ends of the ribbon with the wood-burning tool. If desired, add ribbon to the back side to make the sachet reversible.

5 To use the sachet, slip it between the pillow and the pillow protector case on the underside of the pillow.

in a clutch

Everyone strives to be organized. This trio of patchwork carryalls makes the task especially appealing.

What You'll Need...

- [ ] Scraps of six to eight coordinating heavy cotton fabrics
- [ ] Cotton quilt batting
- [ ] Hook-and-loop tape (optional)
- [ ] Two 8¾×11½ pieces of medium-weight cardboard

pretty organized

The projects measure approximately: wallet, 4×8 inches; jewelry bag, 5×10 inches; portfolio, 10×12 inches. *Note:* The wallet and jewelry bag are made in the same way. The measurements for the jewelry bag are in parentheses.

wallet/jewelry bag

1 For the wallet (jewelry bag), cut and piece the fabrics to make a 9-inch (11-inch) square. Cut a matching piece of batting. Lay the pieced fabric over the batting. Topstitch through all layers ⅛ inch from each side of each seam.

2 Cut a matching square for the lining. Cut two 3½×9-inch (4½×11-inch) inside pockets. Cut a 1½-inch-wide binding strip for each pocket. Press the strips in half lengthwise; press under the long raw edges. Slip a strip over one long edge of each pocket and topstitch it in place, encasing all raw edges.

3 Baste the pockets to the lining piece, aligning the outer edges. See the photographs *above* for details. If desired, topstitch vertically across the pockets to create smaller compartments.

4 With right sides facing and using ½-inch seams, sew the lining to the top. Leave an opening for turning. Trim the seams. Turn, press, and edgestitch all around. If desired, add hook-and-loop strips for closures.

portfolio

1 To make the portfolio, follow the wallet instructions for assembling the top, lining, and pockets using the following measurements: 13×20 inches for the patchwork top, batting, and lining; 8×20-inch patchwork pocket with a 10-inch-wide piece for the right side and pieced sections for the left side. NOTE: Cut the pieced sections to fit items that will be placed in the pockets. See the photograph *top left* for details.

2 Sew the front to the lining as described for the wallet, leaving the top edge open. After turning, slide a piece of cardboard in each side. Fold under the top raw edges and topstitch.

139

in the cards

Take a peek at what's showing through the windows of these cards made with pretty papers and punches.

window views

1 Cut the decorative card stock to measure 8½×5½ inches. Fold the papers in half widthwise to measure 4¼×5½ inches. Punch a square opening in the front of each card ⅞ inch from the top and centered from side to side.

2 Punch a snowman, star, or snowflake from the shimmery card stock. Referring to the photograph *opposite*, use a needle to pierce tiny hanging holes in the punched shapes. For the snowman, use the bottom button as one hole and make the second hole in the hat. For the star and snowflake, punch two holes opposite each other.

3 Center and tape the punches in the windows. Pierce holes close to the window edges so they align with the holes in the punches.

4 Thread the needle with an 8-inch length of thread. Working from the back of the card, sew through the window hole to the front of the card and back through the front of the punch. Tie the thread in a square knot. Repeat for the other holes. Slide the knots so they are positioned behind the card. Place a dot of glue on each knot, trim the thread ends, and remove the tape.

141

What You'll Need...

- [ ] Decorative card stock
- [ ] Paper cutter or scissors and straightedge
- [ ] Paper punches: ¹¹⁄₁₆-inch square, snowman silhouette, jumbo snowflake, jumbo star
- [ ] White, silver, and gold shimmery card stock
- [ ] Clear low-tack tape for paper and framing, such as Scotch 811 tape
- [ ] Needle
- [ ] Silver and gold metallic threads
- [ ] Quick-drying industrial-strength glue

Materials from office supply and scrapbooking stores join forces to make a pretty holiday greeting. Place cardboard and a holiday paper inside a frame. Loop wires around the top loop of a bulldog clip, adding beads. Attach the clip to the framed paper with a brad. Layer smaller pieces of paper for an inset and attach scrapbooking letters to spell out your message. Hold the greeting in place using the bulldog clip.

In a Twinkling:
gifts to give

◀ Shed Some Light: Turn a pretty candlestick into an elegant lamp in a matter of minutes. Shop home improvement stores for candle and bottle adapter kits. Choose the adapter that best fits the candle cup. See the photograph *above* for details. Wire the socket according to the manufacturer's directions, set it inside the candle cup, add a clip-on shade, and voila!—an instant lamp.

Be Jeweled: Turn pretty metal buttons into exotic jewelry. To make a pin, cover the holes by running wire through a bead and then through the button. Punch a hole in the button to add dangling beads. For earrings, glue buttons back-to-back. Run wires through the holes, adding beads above and below the button.

Top It Off: Polymer clay and anodized wires turn corks into clever bottle stoppers. Press a cork into a ball of kneaded polymer clay. Flatten additional balls of clay for the decorative tops, layering, shaping, and stamping them as desired. Add wires between the layers. Join all the layers with polymer adhesive. Stand the corks upright on a baking sheet, stabilizing them with foil. Bake them according to the package directions. After cooling, remove the corks, then glue them back in place with industrial-strength adhesive. Brush the clay with gold metallic acrylic paint.

Tea Light: Look at things from a new perspective with an upside-down tea cup candleholder. Turn the cup upside down and run a bead of silicon sealer around the rim. Press the upright saucer into the sealer so it is level and fits tightly. Let the pair dry overnight. For a festive look, add a bow and some miniature ornaments to the handle and a short, squat pillar candle to the saucer.

144

just for kids

will tell you that getting presents is great,

but making and giving them is even better. Just-for-fun crafting ensures plenty

of bonding time during this hectic season. Even teens will want to participate

in this good, old-fashioned family fun.

JUST *for* KIDS

project: fun!

Be a snow kid for a day in a painted sweatshirt that sports a simplified face across your body and a plaid scarf at your waist.

squeeze-style paint, snip the smallest amount of the tip possible. Make swirls for eyes and a loose sideways V shape for the nose. See the photograph *left* for details.

4 After the black paint dries, pour turquoise paint onto the paper plate. Dip the very tips of the brush into the paint. Tap it onto the plate to remove most of the paint. Using a scrubbing motion that leaves fuzzy edges, rub the paint over the eye swirls.

5 Fill in the nose with orange using long strokes and leaving the open end uneven so the paint looks airbrushed.

snow much fun

6 Make black dots for the mouth in the same manner as the eyes. Remove the poster board. Heat-set the paint using the bottle instructions.

1 Machine-wash and dry the shirt and suiting fabric. Do not use fabric softeners, dryer sheets, or detergents with additives. Iron the shirt. If it has a waistband, cut away the ribbing and hem the lower edge.

2 Cut the poster board to fit inside the shirt and insert it.

3 Pour the black paint into the tip-pen bottle (a small bottle that has narrow metal tips that fit over the end, allowing for a very narrow line). If using

7 Cut two strips of plaid suiting 4 inches wide by the width of the fabric. Sew two short ends together. Stay-stitch ½ inch in from both long ends. Fray the fabric up to the stay stitching. Lay the band over the lower edge of the shirt so the seam is at one side. Topstitch the band in place along the stay stitching. Leave a 1-inch space where the loose ends meet. Tie the loose ends in a knot. Trim and fray the tails.

What You'll Need...

- [ ] White sweatshirt without a ribbed waistband or with the band removed
- [ ] Poster board
- [ ] Jacquard or Deka textile paint in black, turquoise, and orange
- [ ] Tip-Pen paint tip bottles by Plaid or squeeze-style fabric paint with a narrow tip
- [ ] Paper plates
- [ ] Stiff-bristled fabric or stencil brushes
- [ ] ⅓ yard of loosely woven plaid wool-blend suiting fabric

147

What You'll Need...

☐ White crafts foam
☐ Tan felt
☐ Purchased slippers
☐ Plastic shopping bags
☐ Tacky crafts or fabric glue
☐ Plastic eyes
☐ 1-inch-diameter red
  pom-poms
☐ 6 inches of brown cord
☐ Fray-checking liquid

148

reindeer slippers

1 Trace the patterns on *page 156.* Cut four antlers from crafts foam and four ears from felt. Stuff the slippers with plastic bags so they hold their shape while you're working on them.

2 Fold a tuck in each ear as shown on the pattern. Glue the tuck in place, using pins to hold the felt until the glue dries. Glue the antlers to the slippers near the ankle. See the photos *above* and *right* for details. Use pins to hold the antlers in place until the glue dries. Glue an ear at the base of each antler.

3 Glue the eyes to the slippers. Glue pom-pom noses to the slipper toes. Cut two 2- to 3-inch lengths of cord. Shape the cords into a smile on the toe of each slipper and glue the cords in place. Apply a dot of fray-checking liquid to the cord ends.

gift box garland

1 Divide the blocks into three groups of seven each. Paint one group red, one white, and one green. Paint each block a second coat. After the paint is dry, decorate each block to look like a small wrapped package. See the photographs *above* for ideas or look at wrapping paper that has small designs. When the paint dries, spray the blocks with varnish.

2 Wrap a ribbon around each block as if wrapping a package. Tie a bow at the top and trim the ends. Lay out the blocks in a pleasing order. Place two jingle bells between each block and two at each end.

3 Cut 1-yard lengths of the ribbons. Beginning at one end of your garland strand, tie a jingle bell to the ribbon. Add a second bell, then a package. Space the pieces about 3 inches apart and tie them all in place. To tie the packages in place, slide the ribbon underneath the bow and place the knot so it is hidden by the bow. At the end of one length of ribbon, tie on a ribbon of a different color. Continue until all the bells and presents are attached. If desired, add a dot of glue to each bow to keep it tied.

What You'll Need...

- ☐ 21 wooden blocks, 1 inch square
- ☐ Red, green, and white acrylic paint
- ☐ Assorted paintbrushes
- ☐ Gloss spray varnish
- ☐ 22 each of red and green jingle bells or 44 assorted jingle bells
- ☐ 1 spool each of 1/8-inch-wide red, green, and white satin ribbon
- ☐ Tacky crafts glue

What You'll Need...

- ☐ Plastic foam balls: 12 two-inch-diameter and 78 one-inch-diameter
- ☐ Brush-on glitter paint
- ☐ Small paintbrushes
- ☐ Black dimensional paint
- ☐ Flat toothpicks
- ☐ Orange acrylic paint
- ☐ 3 pairs each of red and green infant socks
- ☐ White, red, and green embroidery floss
- ☐ Small trims such as jingle bells, pom-poms, chenille strips, ribbon, and beads
- ☐ Tacky crafts glue
- ☐ Quilting thread
- ☐ Darning needle longer than 2 inches

149

snowman garland

1 Paint each plastic foam ball with glitter paint and let it dry. On each large ball, use dimensional paint to make a smile and eyes. Let the paint dry. For each snowman, paint two toothpicks orange; let dry. Hold the toothpicks together and push them into the ball until the nose is about ¾ inch long.

2 Cut the ribbed portion from the socks, then cut each ribbed portion in half, forming two tubes. Slip a sock half over each snowman to form a hat. Roll or fold the lower edge for a cuff and tie the top with embroidery floss to form stocking caps. Decorate the hats with small trims, chenille strips, and ribbons. See the photograph *right* for ideas.

3 Thread the darning needle with quilting thread but do not cut the thread from the spool. Run the needle through six snowballs, then add a snowman. For the snowballs, run the needle through the center. To keep the snowmen facing forward, push the needle through the upper back of the ball. Repeat to string together all the balls and snowmen. To end the garland, cut the thread, leaving long tails. Loop the thread back and tie it between the first two balls.

Hold fast to dreams
For if dreams die
Life is a broken-winged bird
That cannot fly.
—Langston Hughes

What You'll Need...

- [ ] 3-inch square of
  ⅛-inch-thick acrylic plastic
- [ ] Drill and a small bit
- [ ] Purchased journal with
  a cardboard cover
- [ ] Assorted flat charms,
  trinkets, appliqués,
  photographs, printed
  quotes, and other
  personalized items
- [ ] Assorted beads, including
  one dangle-style bead
  and four identical beads
  for corner spacers
- [ ] Scrapbooking pop dots
- [ ] Archival-quality glue
- [ ] 26-gauge colored wire
- [ ] Gummed linen tape

journalistic style

1 Drill a small hole in each corner of the acrylic plastic square. Use a slow speed and do not remove the protective sheet before drilling. Place the square on the top half of the journal cover. Mark through the holes and onto the cover. Drill holes at the marks. This will form the outline for arranging the decorative elements.

2 Arrange the items within the marks. Allow a few items to extend beyond the perimeter of the square. If any items cover a hole, re-punch the hole. Elevate some items on pop dots. Hold the square over the arrangement and make any needed adjustments. Glue the items into place. Remove the protective plastic from the acrylic plastic square.

3 Cut an 18-inch length of wire. Starting on the inside cover and leaving a long tail, thread the wire through a top hole, a corner bead, and the matching corner of the square. Continue across the top of the square. Run the wire down through the square, a corner bead, and the journal. Draw the wire to the lower hole and repeat the process. String beads along the bottom wire, centering the dangling bead.

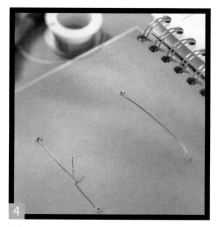

4

When the square is wired in place, pull the wire taut and twist the ends together.

5

Using gummed linen tape, cover the wire on the inside of the journal cover.

6 Add appliqués or charms to the front of the acrylic plastic square, if desired.

What You'll Need...

- ☐ Purchased blue cotton canvas apron
- ☐ Acrylic paint in white and metallic gold and matching textile medium
- ☐ Paintbrushes, including a 1-inch-wide disposable foam brush
- ☐ Dimensional paint in metallic gold, yellow, and white

Hanukkah hands

1 Wash and dry the apron. Do not use fabric softener, dryer sheets, or detergent with additives. Iron the apron. Mix the acrylic paints with textile medium as described on the bottle directions.

Paint a child's fingers and hands from the tips to the center crease with a generous coating of white acrylic paint. The fingers will form the eight candles of the menorah.

With the fingers spread so they are apart but upright, press the child's hands onto the top of the apron. Leave a slight space between the hands for the tall center shamash candle. Wash the paint from the child's hands. Paint both index fingers. Press one finger in the open space between the sets of fingers. Press the second finger above the first one to form the shamash in the center of the menorah.

Outline a flame above each candle using gold dimensional paint. Fill in the flame with yellow paint, swirling the two paints slightly. If desired, brush on small amounts of white paint to make smoke squiggles above the candles.

5 Add names, Happy Hanukkah, Stars of David, and other decorations to the apron using the various paints. Let the paints dry and heat-set them following the manufacturer's directions.

◀ Thrilling Quilling: Update the age-old craft of quilling with curly little trees. Cut construction paper into ¼-inch strips or run it through a paper shredder. Cut a trunk and pairs of long, medium, and short branches. Curl the branches around a toothpick. Uncurl the branches and glue them in place. See the photograph *left* for details. Turn the top on itself to form a hanging loop.

In a Twinkling:
for kids

◀ Clip Art: Display the work of young Picassos with frames featuring clips. For the clipboard frames, sand, prime, and paint clipboards. Add stamped designs. For the bulldog clip frame, replace the clips of a purchased wooden-backed rimless glass frame with colorful bulldog clips. To make a stand, slightly bend a small L-bracket and glue one leg to the back with industrial-strength adhesive. See the photo *above*.

◀ Picture Perfect: Remember your friends and family this season with garlands and ornaments made from crafting foam. Photocopy or print pictures of your favorite people and pets. Cut the foam into frames that fit the pictures. Add stick-on decorations and ribbons or loops for hanging.

153

◀ Brush with Success: Paint your own papers this year for gift wrap like no other. Using a narrow paint roller from the crafts store, make stripes of red acrylic paint across white or brown kraft paper. After the paint dries, add stripes of green to create a plaid design. Cut pop-up sponges into your favorite holiday shapes, making sure they fit within the plaid pattern. Dampen the sponges, wring them dry, and stamp designs onto the paper. Tie the packages with colorful coordinating raffia or ribbon.

patterns

Patterns are 100% size unless otherwise noted. To enlarge patterns, take this book to a copy center and enlarge the pattern using a photocopier.

Each Square = 2 inches

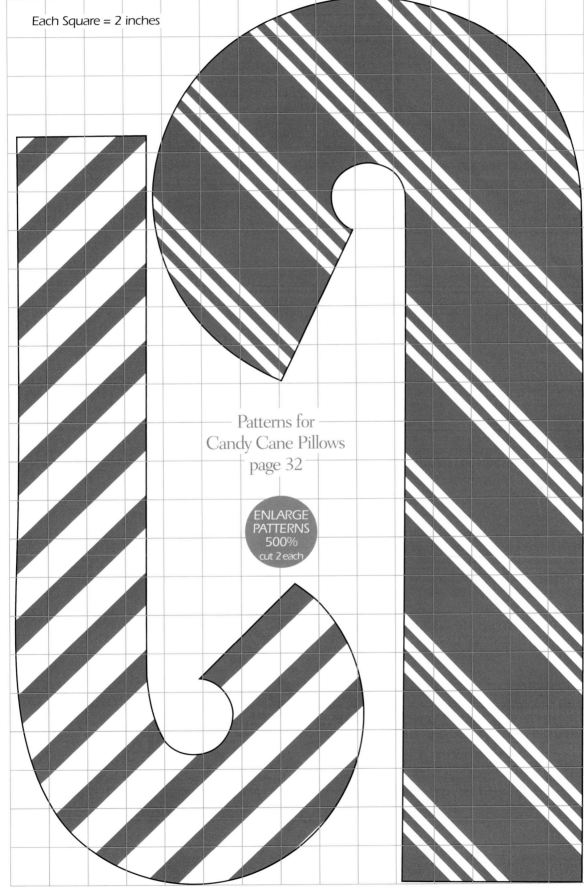

Patterns for
Candy Cane Pillows
page 32

ENLARGE
PATTERNS
500%
cut 2 each

155

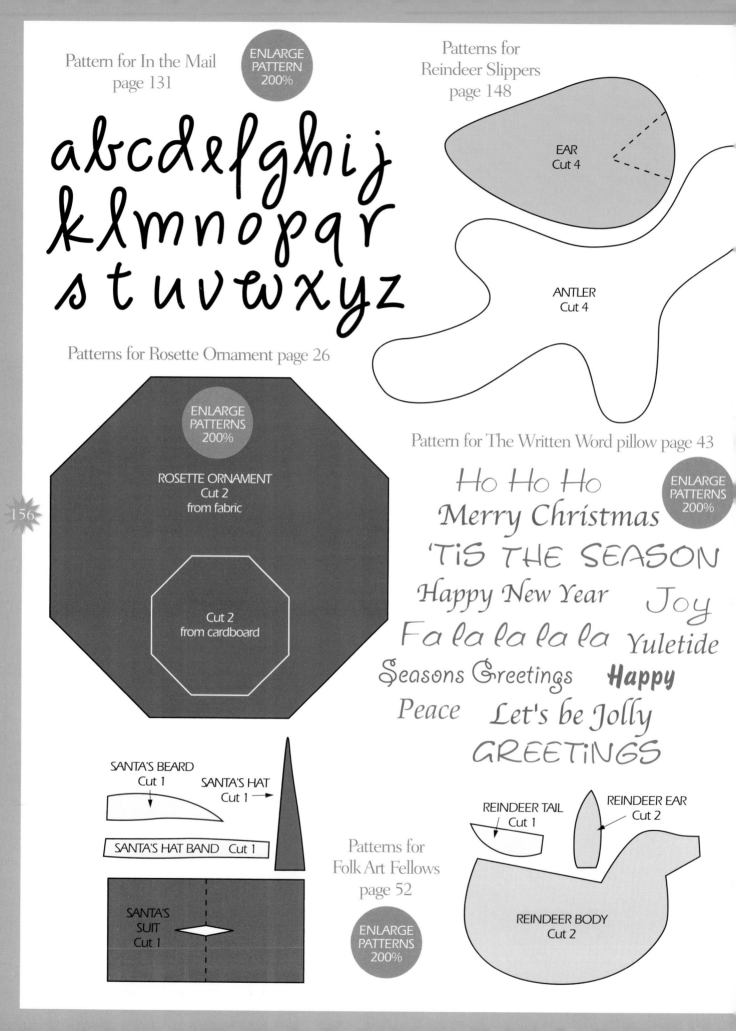

Pattern for In the Mail
page 131

ENLARGE
PATTERN
200%

Patterns for
Reindeer Slippers
page 148

EAR
Cut 4

ANTLER
Cut 4

a b c d e f g h i j
k l m n o p q r
s t u v w x y z

Patterns for Rosette Ornament page 26

ENLARGE
PATTERNS
200%

ROSETTE ORNAMENT
Cut 2
from fabric

Cut 2
from cardboard

156

Pattern for The Written Word pillow page 43

ENLARGE
PATTERNS
200%

Ho Ho Ho
Merry Christmas
'Tis The Season
Happy New Year   Joy
Fa la la la la   Yuletide
Seasons Greetings   Happy
Peace   Let's be Jolly
GREETiNGS

SANTA'S BEARD
Cut 1

SANTA'S HAT
Cut 1

SANTA'S HAT BAND   Cut 1

SANTA'S
SUIT
Cut 1

Patterns for
Folk Art Fellows
page 52

ENLARGE
PATTERNS
200%

REINDEER TAIL
Cut 1

REINDEER EAR
Cut 2

REINDEER BODY
Cut 2

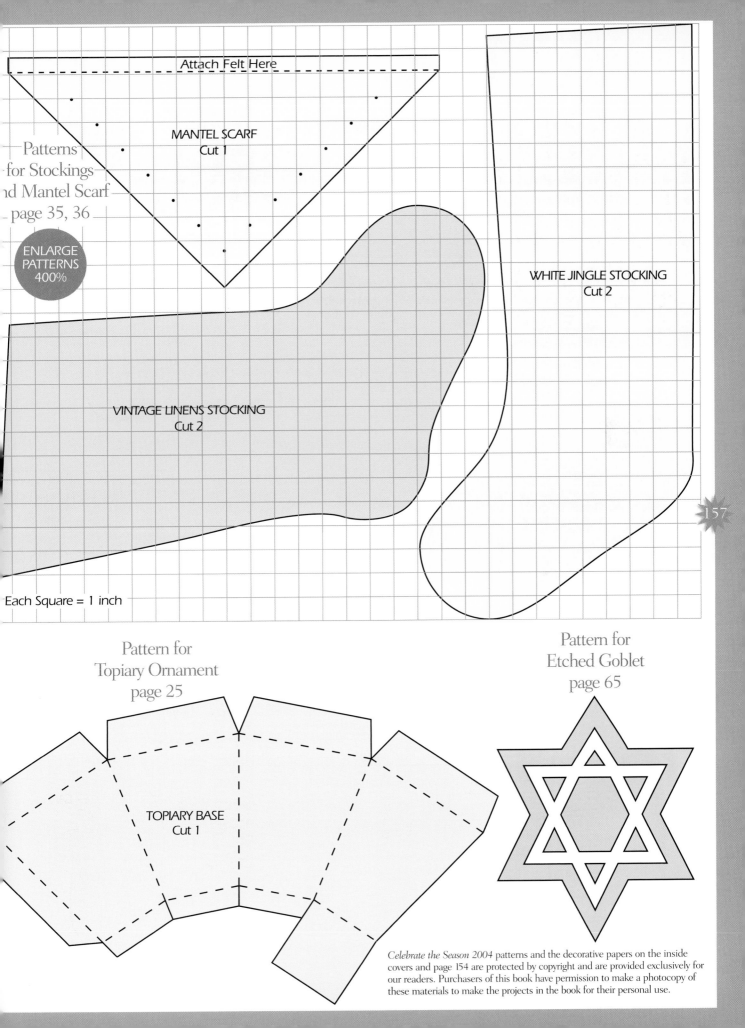

Attach Felt Here

MANTEL SCARF
Cut 1

Patterns
for Stockings
and Mantel Scarf
page 35, 36

ENLARGE
PATTERNS
400%

WHITE JINGLE STOCKING
Cut 2

VINTAGE LINENS STOCKING
Cut 2

Each Square = 1 inch

157

Pattern for
Topiary Ornament
page 25

TOPIARY BASE
Cut 1

Pattern for
Etched Goblet
page 65

Celebrate the Season 2004 patterns and the decorative papers on the inside covers and page 154 are protected by copyright and are provided exclusively for our readers. Purchasers of this book have permission to make a photocopy of these materials to make the projects in the book for their personal use.

credits & sources

Unless otherwise stated, photo styling by Marisa Dirks and Jilann Severson.
Food styling by Charles Worthington and Paige Boyle.
Photographs by Jay Wilde and Marty Baldwin.

cover, page 4: photo, Peter Krumhardt
inside front and back covers: holly paper design, Talathy O'Sullivan
pages 8–11: designs, Jim Williams
pages 12–13: design, Gayle Schadendorf; Ultrasuede® from Field's Fabrics, www.fieldsfabrics.com or call 1-800/678-5872
pages 14–15: design, Jilann Severson; French Leaves #5115 and #5102 from Sisson Imports. To find a retailer near you, call 1-253/939-1520; lampshade and base from Target. For a store near you, check www.target.com or call 1-800/440-0680
pages 16–17: design, Gayle Schadendorf; Suspended Wall Vase #1125897 from Pottery Barn, www.PotteryBarn.com or call 1-800/922-5507; curtain rod and rings from Target. For a store near you, check www.target.com or call 1-800/440-0680
pages 18–19: A Corner on Color wreath design, Jilann Severson; Sheer Genius place mat and Bead It bobeche design, Marisa Dirks; Stick 'em Up magnet, Nesting Season wall hanging, and Picture This pillow designs, Sharon Widdop; images for magnets and pillow from Broderbund Print Shop Deluxe Version 12, available at computer and office supply stores
pages 20–23: designs, Carrie Hanson; photos, Peter Krumhardt
pages 24–27: designs, Mary Jo Hiney Designs; photos, Peter Krumhardt
pages 28–31: photos, John Reed Forsman; shells from The Shell Factory, www.shellfactory.com or call 1-800/282-5805

pages 32–33: designs, Jim Williams
pages 34–37: designs, Suzi Carson
pages 38, 40–41: designs, Jim Williams; photos, Tria Giovan
page 39: design, Mary Jo Hiney Design; photo, Greg Scheidemann
pages 42–43: Gilded Treasure candle ring design, Jim Williams; The Written Word pillow design, Jilann Severson
pages 44–47: designs, Jilann Severson; photos, Peter Krumhardt; Rubber Stampede rubber stamps A2613H Large Snowflake, A2614E Snowflake, A2624B Little Snowflake, A2633E Snowflake Border available at crafts stores nationwide. To find a retailer near you, check www.deltacrafts.com/RubberStampede or call 1-800/632-8386
pages 48–51: designs, Heidi Boyd; photos, Greg Scheidemann
pages 52–53: designs, Suzi Carson
pages 54–55: All That Glitters package design, Marisa Dirks; Tiny Treasure spoon ornament design, Suzi Carson; For Peat's Sake peat pot ornament design, Geri Bauman; A Pretty Pair bell ornament design, Jim Williams; vintage images similar to For Peat's Sake available from www.thevintageworkshop.com
pages 58–59: designs, Carol Linnan
pages 60–61: designs, Carol Linnan
pages 62–63: Stocking Stuffers stocking design, Jim Williams; Naturally Elegant centerpiece design, Peggy Johnston; Naturally Elegant centerpiece photo, Hopkins Associates; Picture Perfect flower and frame design, Wendy Musgrave; Picture Perfect flower and frame photo, King Au, Studio Au
pages 64–67: place mat and napkin design, Mary Jo Hiney Designs; all other designs, Jean Wilson
pages 84–85: designs, Gayle Schadendorf
pages 102–103: invitation, place card, and napkin ring design, Marta Patton; glass marker designs, Gayle Schadendorf
pages 126–127: design, Gayle Schadendorf

page 128: design, Talathy O'Sullivan and Jilann Severson
page 129: design, Suzi Carson
pages 130–131: designs, Kris Horning
page 132: design, Gayle Schadendorf
page 133: design, Gayle Schadendorf; Folk Art acrylic paint from Plaid #467 Italian Sage, #431 French Vanilla, and #765 Porcelain Blue available at crafts stores nationwide
pages 134–137: designs, Jilann Severson; Free & Clear Liquid Laundry Detergent available from Seventh Generation. To find a retailer near you, check www.seventhgeneration.com or call 1-800/456-1191; muslin bags, essential oils, and dried herbs available from The Farmhouse, 1-515/986-3628
pages 138–139: designs, Jim Williams
pages 140–141: designs, Veronica Koh; photo, Greg Scheidemann; square punch from Emagination available at crafts stores nationwide. For a retailer near you, check www.emaginationcrafts.com or call 1-866/238-9770; star, snowflake, and snowman punches from Marvy/Uchida available at crafts stores nationwide. For a retailer near you, check www.uchida.com or call 1-800/541-5877
pages 142–143: Spell It Out frame design, Kristin Detrick; Shed Some Light lamp design, Jilann Severson; Tea Light candleholder design, Geri Bauman; Be Jeweled jewelry design, Kristin Detrick; LaMode buttons #26905 and #26906 available at fabric stores nationwide
pages 146–147: design, Jilann Severson
page 150: design, Marisa Dirks
page 151: design, Molly Hersch
pages 152–153: Thrilling Quilling ornament design, Jilann Severson; Clip Art frame design, Jilann Severson; Picture Perfect garland and ornament design, Jilann Severson
page 154: New Year's paper design, Talathy O'Sullivan

index

decorating projects & gifts

A–E

Advent pockets, 22–23
Advent wreath, 20–21
Appliquéd accessories, 8–11
Apron, Hanukkah, 151

Autumn
  appliquéd accessories, 8–11
  candle rings, 19
  decoupage leaf lampshade, 14–15
  magnets, 19
  nest wall hanging, 19
  pillows, 12–13, 19
  place mats, 10, 18
  vase tieback, 17
  window treatments, 16–17
  wreath, 18

Bottle stoppers, 143
Button ornament, 55

Candle Accessories
  autumn candle rings, 19
  golden leaf candle wreaths, 42
  seashell motif hurricanes, 30
  tea cup candle holders, 143

Candy cane pillows, 32–33
Cards, greeting, 66, 141
Centerpieces
  fruit garland, 63
  gift wrap, 60–61
  ornament, 4
  picture frame, 63
  snowman,
Chair covers, 11, 44–47, 63
Chandelier mobile, eucalyptus, 30–31
Children's crafts and gifts, 147–53
Christmas cards, 141
Christmas, meaning of, 77
Christmas tree themes, 24, 28
Clipboard frames, 152
Coasters, autumn appliqué, 11
Crafting foam ornaments and garland, 153
Cupboard top decorations, 42–43
Curtains, leaf motif, 16–17

Decoupage leaf lampshade, 14–15
Decoupage plate, 128
Detergent, scented, 136
Door decoration, snowflake and icicle, 42
Drawer sachets, 136
Dryer sachets, 137

Eucalyptus chandelier mobile, 30–31

F–K

Frames
  crafting foam, 153
  holiday greeting, 142
  picture clips and clipboard, 152
  as tabletop decoration, 63

Garlands, 63, 149, 153

Gift Wrap
  mailable wraps, 130–31
  ornaments as package toppers, 54
  painted, 153
  tips for, 61

Glass markers, New Year's Eve, 103
Goblet, etched, 65
Greeting cards, 66, 141

Hanukkah, 64–67, 77, 151

Invitations, 66, 102

Jewelry, 143
Jewelry bag, 139
Journal, 150

Kwanzaa, 77, 82–85

L–P

Lamp, made from candlestick, 142
Lampshade, decoupage leaf, 14–15
Linen mist, 135

Magnets, 19
Mailable wraps, 130–131
Mantel scarf, 35

Napkin rings, New Year's Eve, 103
Napkins
  Gelt, 65
  Snowman, 126

Nest wall hanging, 19
New Year's Eve, 96–103

Ornaments
  box-pleated satin, 27
  button, 55
  collectible spoons, 54
  crafting foam frames, 153
  garden peat pot, 55
  as package toppers, 54
  paired with ribbon, 55
  quilled tree, 152
  ribbon pinecone, 26
  rosette, 26–27
  silver and white, 48–51
  starfish, 29
  topiary, 25

Paper quilling, 152
Peat pot ornament, 55
Peppermint stick pillows, 32–33

Pillows
  autumn, 12–13, 19
  Christmas, 32–33, 43

Pillow sachets, 137
Pinecone ornament, 26
Place cards, 67, 85, 103

Place mats
  autumn, 10, 18
  Kwanzaa, 84
  snowman, 126

Plate, decoupage, 128
Poinsettia towels, 129
Portfolio, 139

Q–Z

Quilling, 152

Ramadan, meaning of, 77
Red-and-white Christmas theme, 24–27
Reindeer slippers, 148
Rosette ornament, 26–27
Rugs, 133

Sachets, 136, 137
Santa and Rudolph decoration, 52–53
Satin ornament, 27
Seaside Christmas theme, 28–31
Silver and white ornaments, 48–51
Slipcovers, 11, 44–47, 63
Slippers, reindeer, 148
Snowman family decoration, 58–59
Snowman garland, 149
Snowman place mats and napkins, 126
Snowman sweatshirt, 147
Starfish ornament, 29
Stockings
  Christmas, 34–37
  tabletop, 62
Sweatshirt, snowman, 147

Table runner, autumn appliqué, 9

Tabletop Decorations
  Christmas, 60–63
  Hanukkah, 64–67

Tea cup candleholder, 143
Topiary ornament, 25
Towels, poinsettia, 129

Valence, leaf motif, 16–17

Wallet, 139
Window treatments, 16–17, 42
Wine bottle stoppers, 143
Wine cooler, frozen cranberries used for, 62
Wine glass markers, New Year's Eve, 103
Wine goblet, etched, 65

Wreaths
  Advent wreath, 20–21
  autumn, 18
  winter/Christmas, 38–41, 43

recipes

A–C

Almond Butter Crunch, 120–21
Antipasto Bowl, Marinated 123
Antipasto Kabobs, 98

Appetizers. *See also Antipasto;*
  Caramelized Onion and
    Fig Bruschetta, 98
  Cucumber-Cheese Bites, 122
  Dried Cherry & Green Onion Spread, 123
  Festive Chicken Liver and Pear Spread, 78
  Nutty-Sweet Brie, 123
  Peppery Cream Cheese with Nuts, 122
  Pesto Roll-Ups, 122
  Prosciutto-Wrapped Fruit, 123
  Smoky Cheese Log, 71
  Three-Cheese Spread with Almonds, 105

index *continued*

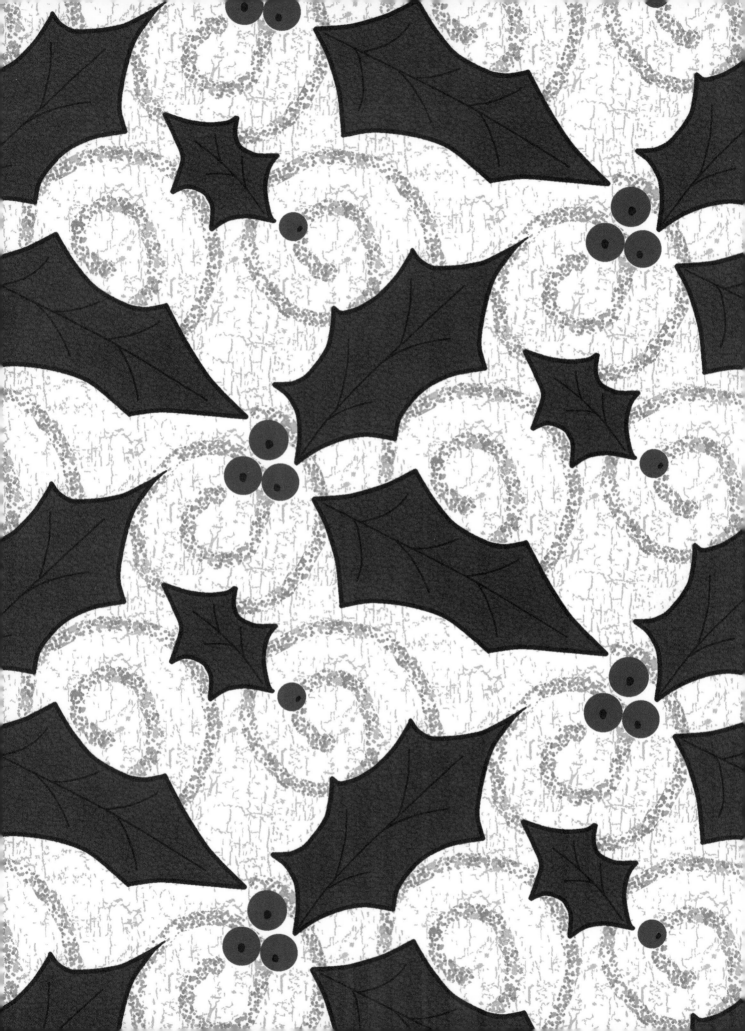